ECOLOGY
and the Bible

FRÉDÉRIC BAUDIN

ECOLOGY
and the Bible

Translated by DAMON DIMAURO

HENDRICKSON
PUBLISHERS

an imprint of Hendrickson Publishing Group

Ecology and the Bible

© 2020 Frédéric Baudin

Translated by Damon DiMauro

Published by Hendrickson Publishers
an imprint of Hendrickson Publishing Group
Hendrickson Publishers, LLC
P. O. Box 3473
Peabody, Massachusetts 01961-3473
www.hendricksonpublishinggroup.com

ISBN 978-1-68307-257-7

Originally published in French under the title: *La Bible et l'écologie*
Copyright © 2013 and 2020 by Frédéric Baudin
Published by permission of Excelsis, 26450 Charols, France
Internet: www.XL6.com

Cover photo by Jasmina007 via Getty Images Plus

Printed in the United States of America

First Printing — July 2020

Library of Congress Control Number: 2020936931

CONTENTS

Introduction   1

1. The Stewardship Mandate and Its Implications   5

2. The Reversal of the Creation Order   21

3. The Laws and Limits of Human Activity   35

4. The Gospel and Protection of the Environment   51

5. Ecology and "New Creation"   67

6. Eschatology and Ecology   79

7. From Theory to Practice   99

8. Christians and Ecology   129

INTRODUCTION

Let's imagine for a moment that a generous patron of the arts asks a couple who are among his close friends to take into their care a masterpiece—perhaps one of Paul Cézanne's (1839–1906) post-Impressionist paintings of Sainte-Victoire, a mountain overlooking Aix-en-Provence in southern France. So great is its value that an insurer has appraised it at over one hundred million dollars. The husband and wife who have been appointed as caretakers now have the responsibility to safeguard this treasure for a time.

Grateful to be entrusted with this painting, they proudly display it in a prominent place in their home where family, friends, and visitors can admire its every detail. They appreciate Cézanne's mastery and his choice of vibrant colors, which he applied to the canvas with awe-inspiring grace. They marvel at his genius, especially his sensitivity to the variations of light over the landscape. They are astonished by his desire to return to this same motif, this mountain he painted so often, this Sainte-Victoire whose forms, beauty, balance—like an imprint of God—he never ceased to explore, even as he sought to capture the bluish flowing hues of its movement toward the sky.

Over time, however, the once delighted caretakers begin to take the painting for granted. They gradually become indifferent to its beauty and even begin to neglect it. They no longer dust the canvas nor close the blinds against the midday sun's harsh light. As a result, the artist's brilliant colors fade and the landscape loses its sheen, becoming dismal and dull.

The caretakers then let their children begin to play on the couch situated just beneath the ornate frame. At first, they sternly admonish them to resist any temptation to damage the painting, warning of dire consequences should they dare even touch it. After a while, however, they barely say a word when their youngest makes a game of pressing jam-covered fingers against the canvas until it stretches and even cracks in certain places, including the mountain's splendid summit. They do become quietly angry, though, when their eldest children begin to throw darts at the green trees and red roofs of the houses at the foot of the mountain, but they end up taking this damage in stride. At last, when their three children, emboldened by their inaction, cover what remains of Sainte-Victoire with dark smudges, they simply sigh and throw up their hands, and they ultimately turn the painting to the wall.

Trying to justify their lack of concern, the father says, "We don't need to bother trying to repair the painting. After all, like all earthly things, it will eventually fade away." The mother then adds, "I think this painting had become almost an object of worship. Too many of us had become overly engrossed in the work itself to the point that the artist himself was no longer fully appreciated." With this, they conclude that they had done well to hide it.

Imagine now that the original owner of the painting returns to reclaim Cézanne's masterpiece. What should be his reaction when he sees what has become of it? His anger, his righteous indignation against the negligent caretakers, would be understandable. He thinks about taking them to court over the cost of the ruined painting, but then another generous lover of the arts offers to restore the entire painting at his own cost. Thanks to this providential mediator, the owner no longer needs to prosecute the couple he had entrusted with the safekeeping of the grand master's work. He even allows it to remain with them, since they seem to sincerely regret their negligence. They promise to watch over the painting until the owner is ready to take it back—though he does wonder if he can trust them after this.

Although the anecdote here might seem far-fetched, it should be obvious that we are really talking about God's creation—and how we have neglected his masterpiece, this earth. In our capacity as free and responsible human beings, we have been mandated by the Creator to care for his creation. Like our story with a new art lover willing to restore the painting, however, perhaps it is not too late to fulfill our original mandate.

Since Jesus—our generous benefactor—has indeed redeemed our world (although we are still awaiting the final fulfillment from him), there is still time for us to be witnesses of the firstfruits of this restoration and hope by taking care of our planet in these latter days with faith and with love—toward both the Creator and his creation.

1

THE STEWARDSHIP
MANDATE AND ITS
IMPLICATIONS

God blessed them and said to them, "Be fruitful and
increase in number; fill the earth and subdue it. Rule
over the fish in the sea and the birds in the sky and over
every living creature that moves on the ground."

(Gen. 1:28)

In the Bible, several different verbs are used to delineate the
responsibilities of men and women created by God: they are en-
joined "to multiply and fill" the earth, "to rule and have dominion
over" the animals, the vegetation, and natural resources broadly
speaking, and finally, "to till and keep" the "garden."

The verbs in Genesis 1:28 do not pose any real difficulty in
translation: *pārāh* signifies "to bear fruit," "to be fruitful," and
hence "to reproduce"; *rābā* is most often translated as "to multiply," "to increase" (i.e., in number); *mālēh'* is in general rendered
faithfully by the verb "to fill" (i.e., in order to populate the earth).
Only *kābaš*, "to subjugate," and *radâ*, "to rule over" might war-
rant more nuance and subtlety in translation, for we shall see that
their meaning is less pejorative in this particular context than
might be imagined at first glance. All of these verbs are in the
imperative mood, as they are in several other creation-related
passages (Gen. 1:22, 28; 9:1, etc.). What has been generally termed
the "stewardship mandate" is thus a command, addressed by God
to humankind.

Populating the Earth

The divine blessing that accompanies the stewardship mandate recurs ten times in the book of Genesis, both before and after the flood, for animals (Gen. 1:22), as well as for humans (Gen. 1:28; 8:17; 9:1, 7) and more pertinently the offspring of Abraham (Gen. 17:20; 28:3; 35:11; 47:27; 48:4). This blessing concerns, in the first instance, the capacity for the male-female pair to be fruitful. It does not mitigate the need for birth control, but rather frames population growth in a positive perspective for humankind.

Nevertheless, since the dawn of human history, population growth has long been regulated (which has been the occasion, alas, of great suffering as well) by natural disasters, epidemics, high rates of infant mortality, and human conflict. Humans have sometimes modified significantly their environment (through the expansion of agriculture during the Neolithic period, the controlled use of fire, animal husbandry and herding, land clearing, and agricultural development in the Middle Ages, etc.), but they never seriously came to question natural balances on a planetary scale until the modern era.

The Demographic Shift

World population thus remained relatively stable or was marked by low and slow growth, rising only from 250 million to 950 million between the first century after Christ and the end of the eighteenth century—though the average life expectancy never exceeded 25 to 30 years from one place and epoch to another.

The makings of a demographic shift can be perceived as early as the Industrial Revolution in Europe and North America (1750–1850). This shift began with a decline in mortality rates due to progress on several fronts: medicine; the widespread adoption of hygienic practices; the development of agriculture, industry, and transportation; and better nutrition. These factors all favored both successful birthrates (a steep decline in infant mortality before age one) and life expectancy. Although the population greatly increased over the course of several decades, the birthrate soon declined in turn as populations modified their behavior ("natural" contraception and then "artificial" when the pill became available in 1960), employing all possible means to maintain this new "comfort level" of life. It seems as though the inordinate fear of "losing" this level of comfort, linked to that of not being able to adequately raise more children, reinforced this decline all the more.

The demographic pattern that followed this shift tended then toward a slow natural increase due to a very low birthrate, indeed insufficient to ensure generational renewal. This is most often the case today in Europe, North America, and Japan where the fertility rate (the average number of children per woman of childbearing age) ranged from 1.4 to 1.9 in 2019 (2.5 on the global scale), thus two times less than in 1950. In these nations, the population is aging (life expectancy is the highest in the world), raising the prospect of economic and social problems on the horizon, such as pension funding, social assistance, medical care for the elderly, and decreased productivity, shortage of labor, and loss of dynamism for society as a whole. Immigration can compensate in part for these deficiencies, but certain countries, such as Japan, have been resistant to it until recent years.

A phased demographic shift lasted for about a century in Europe and North America, but it was more accelerated in countries that developed more recently, such as in Asia where Taiwan, Singapore, and South Korea hold the record for the lowest fertility rate in the world (1.2 child per female). This shift is far from taking hold in many other countries, however, most notably in Africa. In certain parts of Southeast Asia, the distribution of men and women is unequal (with a birth imbalance of up to 48% of females versus 52% of males). This is because a form of eugenics is being practiced in certain countries (prenatal diagnosis and abortion, if not infanticide) with a view to limiting the number of female births, mainly for cultural reasons (such as excessive honor placed on the birth of a boy) and for financial reasons (payment of a dowry on the occasion of the marriage of a girl).

The Demographic Explosion
and its Consequences

At the beginning of the nineteenth century, economist and Anglican priest Thomas Robert Malthus (1766–1834) became concerned about the divide between the growth of population on the one hand and the availability of resources on the other. It is estimated that world population numbered from 900 million to one billion people at the time and that life expectancy hovered between 30 and 35 years of age. By 1930, this figure had doubled (two billion people), then it climbed to four billion in 1975, and then to six billion in 2000. It is estimated today (2019) that the population has risen to 7.7 billion people and that life expectancy at birth is about 72 years of age (about 80 in Europe, North America, Australia, and New Zealand; from 70 to 77 in other countries of Oceania, Asia, Latin America, and North Africa; and 50 to 65 in sub-Saharan Africa and other African countries).

This "demographic explosion" is partially to blame for the deterioration of the environment. In effect, in order to sustain populations in rapid expansion, it became necessary to develop agriculture and industry, and then to ensure the large-scale distribution of processed foods. Housing was developed and various infrastructures were put in place to welcome families and support men and women at work, and the networks of transportation and communication were extended. These *critical* measures drove strong growth in the production and consumption of energy, as well as in obvious pollution, thus disrupting numerous ecosystems of the planet.

Concerning food production, the situation is uneven in the world. In certain regions, malnutrition is still a reality, in particular in sub-Saharan Africa. Famine remains a threat whenever climatic conditions become unfavorable or, more often, whenever armed conflict breaks out. Famine occurs as well whenever aid is poorly distributed and, in certain cases, becomes a political weapon linked to corruption among the elite, which reveals itself, in the final analysis, to be one of the main obstacles to development. By contrast, in "developed"[1] countries, the threshold of basic well-being has largely been surpassed, even if some individuals do not always benefit from this prosperity. Economic growth cycles alternate according to crises of varying severity.

The rate of annual population growth reached its peak between 1965 and 1970 (about 2%). It has since then regularly decreased, but it remains sufficient for world population to continue to increase (about 1.2% in 2019). According to the most realistic (and average) projections, it is estimated that world population could hit eight to ten billion before the end of the 21st century. It should decrease then, when the demographic shift runs its course on a global scale (see the world population clock on the following site: www.ined.fr/en).

From now until 2050, the fertility rate is expected to decline from 2.5 to 2.2 children per woman and life expectancy to increase from 72 to 77. No one can say what will be the specific migration patterns, notably for "climatic" reasons and undoubtedly more often following political conflicts. For example, between 2010 and 2020, some fifteen countries or regions in the world have seen an inflow of over a million migrants, while a dozen or so lost their population in the same proportions.

On the basis of current indices (fertility and birthrates, life and death expectancy), projections show that during this period (2020–2050), the populations of European countries and Japan will decline, at times drastically (Japan lost about 500,000 inhabitants in 2018,

---

[1] In principle, a distinction is drawn, according to economic criteria, between developed countries (or "high income") and developing countries (or "middle income," subdivided into upper and lower, and from which "emerging countries" with a recent and rapid development are separated) and the least developed countries (or "low income"), whose development is slower and more precarious. The Human Development Index (HDI), drawn up by the United Nations Development Programme (UNDP), adds qualitative criteria such as level of health (life expectancy linked to medical conditions, hygiene, and food, etc.) and education (school attendance and literacy, access to culture, etc.), which qualify somewhat this "prize list."

which will increase to 25 million at this pace within a half century); while in sub-Saharan African countries, populations will double (and even triple in Niger), although the average number of children per woman will slowly decline. In other African countries—as well as in Yemen, Afghanistan, and Pakistan—growth will remain strong (more than 50%). Growth will be lower in other Middle Eastern countries and in Central and Latin America; while moderate growth will continue in North America, Asia, and North Africa.

China and India present a special case: China will have roughly 1.4 billion inhabitants in 2050, "only" 30 million fewer than in 2019; while India will gain almost 300 million and will rapidly become the most populated country in the world. The most dramatic development (and worrisome if current trends continue) remains that of the African continent, whose population will increase from one billion in 2010 to about 2.3 billion in 2050, thus 50% of worldwide growth according to United Nations estimates. In Nigeria, the most densely populated country in Africa, the increase will be from 200 to 400 million, which will make it probably more populous than the United States.[2]

Sustainable Development

It seems possible to feed this population, provided that no major upheavals take place, such as a natural disasters, epidemics, industrial accidents, or political conflicts. The challenge today, then, is to find agricultural, industrial, urban, and energy solutions that cause the least amount of damage to the environment. At the same time, we must be able to feed and house in the most efficient way possible the greatest number of individuals, without stifling economic, technological, scientific, and social progress.

Now, this is a definition of "development" that can rightly be qualified by the adjective "sustainable." The expression "sustainable

---

[2] See World Population Prospects 2019: https://population.un.org/wpp/Download/Standard/Population/.

development" was first coined in 1980 by the International Union for Conservation of Nature (IUCN). It made its way into everyday usage in 1987 when Gro Harlem Brundtland, then prime minister of Norway and president of the World Commission on Environment and Development, published her report *Our Common Future*, also known as the "Brundtland Report."

This report states that present development must not jeopardize future development, and that it must permit succeeding generations to live in optimal conditions of comfort and to avail themselves of the natural resources necessary for their well-being:

> The human race has the full means to render development sustainable, so as to meet the needs of the present without compromising the ability of future generations to meet theirs. The concept of sustainable development does imply limits—not absolute limits but those imposed by the present state of technology and social organization on environmental resources as well as by the capacity of the biosphere to absorb the effects of human activity.[3]

The ideal thus defined is highly ambitious, but it is also constrained by man-made and natural hazards that continue to arise—and most especially by the irrational and insatiable appetites of those who wish to wield excessive power and accumulate the goods of this world, which the Bible makes a point of condemning.

An Abusive Dominion

In Western societies, development has resulted in an overreaching manipulation, an almost unbridled exploitation of all-natural resources, and the consequences of this overexploitation have sometimes been dramatic.

---

[3] *Our Common Future: The World Commission on Environment and Development* (Oxford: Oxford University Press, 1987), I.3.

It is not right that yield concerns, which have a certain legitimate merit, should drive farmers and ranchers, for example, to exceed the laws of nature by using massive amounts of synthetic fertilizers and pesticides, meat-and-bone meal, antibiotics, and growth hormones. It is not necessarily the use in itself of these means that is ill-considered or reprehensible, but rather the systematic recourse to them without critical reflection or adequate precautions, and oftentimes even without restraint. These instances include the heavy spraying of an organochlorine insecticide, known as chlordecone, which was used for over twenty years in the French West Indies to combat banana weevils (1972–1993, though officially until 1990), although it was banned in the United States as early as 1976. The health consequences are significant and often tragic: soils have been contaminated for several hundreds of years, and a higher cancer rate, especially prostate cancer in men, has been found among the communities directly affected. In certain cases, it is possible to do without these products, or at the very least to find fertilizers and more "natural" means of control, which are just as efficient to nourish plants and fight bacteria or insects. This point is borne out more and more every year by the success of "organic" farming (that uses neither synthetic fertilizer nor pesticide) and "integrated" farming (with its more holistic approach of managing health risks, work safety, and animal welfare).

It is patently untenable to use the formidable power of machines to lay waste to natural space without restraint. Since 1850, about 10 million square kilometers have been cleared and converted, most often to meet the needs of increased population and urbanization. In developing countries, moreover, space management has not always been optimized. The rural exodus and the concomitant growth of cities raise serious questions about the future of populations living in either these deserted or now congested spaces.

The dependence of humans on our favorite mode of transportation does not cease to increase: the automobile, symbol and instrument of our freedom, is without doubt one of the crown jewels of our technological civilization, but the enslavement to convenience it offers ends up becoming a net negative. Growth patterns have swung in many different directions—residential, commercial, industrial, recreational, etc.—precisely because the automobile was counted upon as the preferred means of transportation. Human beings are walking less and less, whether going from our residence to school or the workplace, whether doing errands or getting to church. In certain cases, walking has even become the exception!

While travel on foot was still common fifty or so years ago, it is astonishing to see how much has changed within these past decades. Automobile traffic is omnipresent, creating traffic jams and pollution of every kind: toxic greenhouse gases, noise and odors, not to mention accidents and their often-fatal consequences. And what about the seasonal invasion of tourists in the mountains or on the coasts, which leaves an undesirable (and often lasting) mark on nature? It is ironic that lovers of natural open spaces tend to invade them by the tens of thousands and end up disfiguring them! Wild flora and fauna are the big losers from these human leisure activities.

Lastly, it is not rational that industrialization should continue to develop without concern for the pollution generated by it. Some sites have been completely defaced, spoiled, or laid waste by the lethal power of pollution that touches every living thing.

Nature Threatened

There have been 1.2 million animal species identified worldwide, in addition to 520,000 plant species (plants and mushrooms), and 3,000 protozoa (single-celled organisms). In actuality, it is estimated that the earth contains between 2 and 8 million species. This means that many species remain yet to be identified and studied, which would require the work of thousands of specialists (taxonomists) for many centuries.

The most species-rich habitats are, nevertheless, threatened; and in particular those in tropical rainforests, which are located most often in developing countries, where they are being reduced by several thousand acres per day. Land-clearing by fire, whether intentional or accidental, is common and contributes to the deple-tion of natural habitats. In total, the *net* loss worldwide (on balance between deforestation and reforestation) is estimated at more than 50,000 square kilometers per year (see, for example, the *National Working Group for Tropical Forests Report*). The negative impact of deforestation is well known: there is erosion and the loss of fertile soils; the climate is affected by greenhouse gases (which can be combated with CO_2 storage), pollution (air and water purifica-tion), and biodiversity (especially in the primary tropical forests). It is said that two to three species of fauna or flora disappear each day; in fact, 57,000 animals and 225 plants are thought to have al-ready "disappeared." Some of these plants, let it be duly noted, very likely contained the necessary elements for the manufacture of new medicines.

According to the "Red List" established by the International Union for Conservation of Nature (IUCN), some 20,000 to 25,000 species are directly threatened (albeit to varying degrees), including 13% of the birds, 25% of the mammals, 27% of the freshwater fish, 41% of the amphibians, and between 40% and 70% of the plants of one species or another (though, in particular, conifers). The study remains still incomplete, however; for it concerns only those 90,000 species that are known and have been identified (see www.iucn.org).

The principal causes of premature extinction are not hard to identify: demographic pressures, industrial and residential sprawl, deforestation and the intensive draining of marshlands (which are habitats of great biological diversity), and excessive agricul-tural practices, not to mention the bad habits and carelessness of human beings. It would be wise and prudent not to engage in finger-pointing here, especially with respect to our predecessors. What would we have done in the same situation and in the same historical context?

Some might argue that there should have been a more rapid response to the population growth of the twentieth century. This, however, is merely trying to avoid engaging now in a radical critique of current demographic and economic growth, and their harmful effects on both humanity and nature. The issue is not an easy one to resolve, given the scale of the demographic boom. We must hear the cries of alarm and understand the anxiety—the anguish—of the younger generations who see our planet being abused by human beings. But it is prudent and wise not to fall into a simplistic analysis and guilty criticism that would be aimed exclusively at previous generations. What would we have done in the same situation and in the same historical context? This state of affairs can nevertheless spur us to delve further into and more accurately interpret the meaning of the words of Genesis.

Dominion: The Care for Creation

Then God said, "Let us make mankind in our image, in our likeness, so that they may rule over the fish in the sea and the birds in the sky, over the livestock and all the wild animals, and over all the creatures that move along the ground." (Gen. 1:26)

According to the Genesis account, men and women were invited to fill, rule, and cultivate the earth *in communion with God*, as befitting beings created *in his image* (Gen. 1:26), endued with a capacity to comport themselves in thought and deed with love and justice. It was not for them a matter of exercising a kind of tyranny over creation, but rather of *caring for* it with a view toward the well-being of all creatures and for the greater glory of the Creator.

Indeed, "to care for" is one of the meanings of the Hebrew verb *radâ*, which is otherwise translated as "to rule over." This verb is employed seven times in the Pentateuch (the first five books of the Bible), including two times in Genesis in a positive sense (1:26, 28). It refers elsewhere to a military conquest by the people of Israel (Num. 24:19) or its opposite: the domination by her enemies after a defeat (Lev. 26:17). In other cases, it appears in a negative command ("Thou shalt not rule . . .") in order to condemn an overbearing control, an abuse of power possibly conjoined with a certain ruthlessness (Lev. 25:43, 46, 53).

The descendants of Abraham were not to "rule" over their brothers in an arbitrary manner. Their rule was exercised in a restricted legislative framework (see Lev. 25 and 26). These laws were given in order to avoid the problems of slavery or, at the very least, to set limits to servitude. When Jews entered into the service of another Jewish family, following a personal bankruptcy, they could be redeemed by a member of their own family (as Ruth, in Scripture, was bought back by Boaz). They also had the possibility, if they so wished, to regain their freedom during a sabbatical year once every seven years (Exod. 21:2), or at the Jubilee that was celebrated every fifty years (Lev. 25:39–40).

The prophets Isaiah, Jeremiah, and Ezekiel reminded kings and religious leaders on several occasions that they needed to exercise dominion with benevolence and justice. Their calling was to care for their people, to conduct themselves as a shepherd would oversee his flock, and not as a power-hungry tyrant as seen in Ezekiel 34:4: "You have not strengthened the weak or healed the sick or bound up the injured. You have not brought back the strays or searched for the lost. You have *ruled* them harshly and brutally" (the verb *radâ* is employed here in the original).

In a positive sense, the Hebrew verb *radâ* implies that man and woman must exercise their dominion over the earth as befitting beings created in the image of God, and that they should consider their function as that of caretakers. The Greek translation of the Bible (the Septuagint) renders the verb *radâ* by *archô*, which indicates an ability to command and to assume the role of a leader (see Mark 10:42), with all its requisite qualities!

The text of Genesis 1:28 does not suggest a tense relationship between two adversaries, as if the world were *a priori* hostile to human beings. Quite the opposite: man and woman were called to bring within their purview domesticated animals and natural resources, so as to better tend fields, operate mines, manage forests (in particular for construction). They would then be able to fulfill their mandate for the greater good and in a sustainable manner.

In Psalm 8, the psalmist echoes the text of Genesis, employing here the verb *mashal* ("to govern") to better illustrate the nature of this rule, a "reign" that consists in evincing wisdom and understanding and that impacts the entire world:

> You have made them a little lower than God and crowned them with glory and honor. You have given them dominion [literally, "you made them rulers"] over the works of your hands; you have put all things under their feet, all sheep and oxen, and also the beasts of the field. (Ps. 8:5–7)

Subjugating: Good Management

The Hebrew verb *kābaš* has led to the most unfortunate and destructive misinterpretations for the natural environment, signifying "to subdue" in the strongest sense—"to subjugate." In the Scriptures, this word was often employed in a pejorative sense to condemn, for example, an abuse of power, as when the Israelites wrongfully pressed their brethren into slavery (2 Chron. 28:10–11; Neh. 5:5; Jer. 34:11, 16). It also suggested sexual violence (Esther 7:8).

Yet the verb *kābaš* has the positive meaning of "to take possession of" (cf. the Septuagint: *katakurieúô*, "to take command of"). This is also how it is understood in the languages close to Hebrew, in ancient Middle East literature, such as on the stele (a stone or wooden slab) of Thutmose III, the sixth pharaoh of the Egyptian Eighteenth Dynasty (1458–1425 BCE) in Karnack, and in the letter of the Assyrian king Sargon II (722–705 BCE). In both cases, the sovereign gave authorization to one of his underlings to "subjugate" his territory so as to administer it in his name. Such is likewise the case in Hebrew for the Israelites who conquered the land of Canaan. The families of Gad and Reuben were able to settle in the occupied lands beyond the Jordan, after having allowed the other families of Israel to *subjugate* the conquered peoples (Num. 32:22, 29; Josh. 18:1).

In the context of Genesis, then, these two Hebrew verbs *mashal* and *kābaš* signify that man and woman are called to superintend creation, to manage it properly, with the knowledge and the skill that God granted them in the exercise of their mandate:

The first chapter [of Genesis] emphasizes the subjection of creation. This fragile being [man] is called to an extraordinary destiny: to exercise "kingship" in God's name over all creation. Neither divine being, nor beast, he is the overseer, the treasurer, and the viceroy of the LORD. However, the second chapter adds an important nuance to the creational mandate, as if to prevent any abuse in its discharge. It is not a matter of imposing a tyranny on creation, but rather of performing a service. When man tills the land, it is his vocation to take care of what God has entrusted to him: he thereby "worships" and serves God in the work he undertakes.[4]

To Till and Keep

The Lord God took the man and put him in the Garden of Eden to work it and take care of it. (Gen. 2:15)

Beyond their literal sense (to till the land for food), in Hebrew, the verbs *'ābad* ("to till," "to labor," "to serve") and *šamar* ("to keep," "to watch over," "to protect") have a religious connotation. The semantic link is not always obvious, but it is not farfetched to read in the broader meaning of these verbs an encouragement to consider human activity in more than mere material terms.

According to the context, in fact, the verb "to till" may signify "to serve God" or "to worship God" (Exod. 3:12; 12:3). It is used to describe the activity of Levites in the temple (Num. 3:7–8; 4:30, 41, 47; 8:11, 15, 19, etc.), for the priests were responsible for "guarding" the sanctuary, and in particular for safeguarding the purity of the holy place, so as to preserve it from all worldly defilement (Exod. 8:35; Num. 1:53). The people of Israel, in return, were called to "keep" the commandments (Exod. 12:2), God's covenant (Gen.

---

[4] Pierre Berthoud, *En quête des origines. Les premières étapes de l'histoire de la Révélation: Genèse 1 à 11* (Charols, France: Excelsis, 2008), 226.

17:9; Exod. 19:5), the Sabbath (Exod. 31:13–14), their souls (i.e., conscience, inner being that can be in relation/communion with God; Deut. 4:9; Prov. 4:21), and religious festivals (Exod. 23:15). In these texts, the verb "to keep" has quite obviously a religious dimension.

These verbs in Genesis signify therefore that the authority delegated by God to human beings—namely, their calling to fill the earth and to till the land, and to identify, name, and protect living creatures—must be exercised *within the limits* of the agricultural mandate commanded by the Creator from the beginning. This mandate remains in spite of the "fall," or the breaking of the covenant between God and humankind. The dominion of man and woman over nature involves not only their worldly activities and responsibilities but also their religious duties.

2

THE REVERSAL OF THE
CREATION ORDER

The Apostles' Creed begins with these words: "I believe in God, the Father almighty, creator of heaven and earth." Thus Christians, like the adherents of the other main monotheistic religions, have a specific vision of the world that influences their relationship with God, as well as with the world that surrounds them—their *environment*.

The book of Genesis, as its name clearly shows, is concerned with "origins"—God's creation—followed by an account of the "ordering" of all things created. The crowning moment of this creation is the appearance on the scene of man and woman, who are made by God "in his image." They are endowed by their Creator with reason (i.e., intelligence, reflection, knowledge, discernment), so that they might exercise this faculty while simultaneously respecting the ethical parameters (i.e., love and justice) of the divine mandate.

The Sowing of Disorder

This remarkable creation narrative, crafted with care,[1] next unveils the drama of the Garden of Eden. Man and woman are

---

[1] See Henri Blocher, *In the Beginning: The Opening Chapters of Genesis*, trans. David G. Preston (Leicester, UK: Inter-Varsity Press, 1984), and Matthieu Richelle, *Comprendre Genèse 1–11 aujourd'hui*, Collection La Bible et son message (Charols-Vaux-sur-Seine: Excelsis-Edifac, 2013).

permitted to gather all the fruits of the trees and of the plants in the garden, which they are charged with "cultivating and keeping," except one alone: the tree of "the knowledge of good and evil." Located in the center of the garden, its fruits are a delight to the eyes and yet they can become deadly. Tempted by a subtler—*craftier*—being, man and woman do not resist this scintillating enticement. They end up picking the fruit that they so desire, and they partake of it without a second thought.

Through this highly emblematic move, they lay claim to their *autonomy*: they want to set their own laws in deciding for themselves what is right and wrong, so as "to be like the gods." By their rebellion, they break the covenant made with the Lord of creation, which is based on mutual trust. They thereby lose the freedom and the contentment they had living in communion with God. This affects their relationships, not only with God but also with one another and with nature. The work of man and woman now becomes toilsome: thorny bushes and shrubs invade the garden, which is now more difficult to cultivate and maintain, and the pains of labor—of childbirth—are increased. Henceforth, the living conditions of human beings become precarious, since they have allowed disorder to take root in the world, disrupting and disturbing their environment. Somehow, they will have to reorient themselves back to the path that leads to the "garden" of the presence of God, whose temple will later become, first in the desert and then in Jerusalem, a symbolic image; they will have to regain access to the tree of life in order to escape death. But the more they distance themselves from God, the less they will be able to care for what he has created.

The reverse is also true: in principle, the more man and woman draw closer to God, the more they will be concerned to take care of what he has created. In Genesis 9:1, the mandate that God established in the garden is extended after the flood. Reconciliation with the Creator remains possible on the earth, at least in part, for the Lord stands ready to renew his covenant and reveal himself to the beings he has created in his image.

Common Revelation

Since what may be known about God is plain to them, because God has made it plain to them. For since the creation of the world God's invisible qualities—his eternal power and divine nature—have been clearly seen, being understood from what has been made, so that people are without excuse. For although they knew God, they neither glorified him as God nor gave thanks to him, but their thinking became futile and their foolish hearts were darkened. Although they claimed to be wise, they became fools and exchanged the glory of the immortal God for images made to look like a mortal human being and birds and animals and reptiles. (Rom. 1:19–23)

The Bible teaches that God is one, invisible and immaterial, personal and distinct from his creation, sovereign and alone worthy to be adored, served, and worshiped (Exod. 20; Deut. 6). If God and nature are not to be confused (which is tantamount to pantheism), creation nevertheless bears the mark of its author, or his personal "signature," so to speak. This is what the apostle Paul suggests at the beginning of his Epistle to the Romans where he harkens back to a number of psalms and other texts of the Old Testament. At times, some speak here of "natural theology"; but the expression is ambiguous, for God's self-revelation in nature remains fragmentary and obscured by human "unrighteousness" (which is the failure to render unto God his due—namely, the honor based on the acknowledgment that he is the author and master of creation). Although men and women made in the image of God might recognize in nature the vestiges of God through his handiwork (common revelation), they cannot clearly see in it the plan of salvation for humanity and for the earth as a whole (special revelation).

Many are those in the world, even if they do not share the Christian faith, who have an intimation of this common revelation. Some marvel quite simply, perhaps naively (no harm in that!), at the display of beauty in nature; others are moved by the wondrous reality of conditions favorable to life on earth in all of its richness and diversity. Some scientists, benefiting from the latest and most advanced technologies, become convinced that this world has a divine origin as they contemplate the subtle ballet of the galaxies, the movement of the stars and of our bluish planet in the universe, regulated by intangible physical constants and an "organized chaos"; they probe the intricacies of the most complex biological mechanisms, such as those concerning the birth of a human being. It is evident to them that the world is not a result of blind chance and deterministic forces! Nevertheless, science alone cannot demonstrate the existence of God.

On numerous occasions, the Bible states that livestock and crops are to be raised and protected by human beings, handled with care in time of peace (e.g., Exod. 23:19 prohibits sacrificing an unweaned animal at the same time as its mother, and Deuteronomy 22:6–7 warns against collecting the eggs or the chicks nestled by their mother), as well as in time of war (e.g., Deut. 20:18–20 prohibits cutting down fruit trees during a siege in enemy territory). The animals are associated with Noah and his family, just as the animals of the city of Nineveh are associated with its inhabitants, to escape God's judgment (Gen. 9; Jon. 3:7; 4:11). Images of plant and animal life are often offered as models in a metaphoric sense (e.g., the diligent activity of ants, the sense direction of migratory birds, the whitening of the harvest, the majesty of the cedar rising to the heights, the flower of the fields better cloaked than King Solomon, etc.). Even farming techniques are inspired by God for human beings to discover and put into practice, as a testimony to his revelation through creation:

> Listen, and hear my voice; pay attention, and hear my speech. Do those who plow for sowing plow continually? Do they continually open and harrow their ground? When they have leveled its surface, do they not scatter dill, sow cumin, and plant wheat in rows and barley in its proper place, and spelt as the border? For they are well instructed; their God teaches them. Dill is not threshed with a threshing sledge, nor is a cart wheel

rolled over cumin; but dill is beaten out with a stick, and cumin with a rod. Grain is crushed for bread, but one does not thresh it forever; one drives the cart wheel and horses over it, but does not pulverize it. This also comes from the Lord of hosts; he is wonderful in counsel, and excellent in wisdom. (Isa. 28.23–29)

Divine Revelation and Human Conscience

Indeed, when Gentiles, who do not have the law, do by nature things required by the law, they are a law for themselves, even though they do not have the law. They show that the requirements of the law are written on their hearts, their consciences also bearing witness, and their thoughts sometimes accusing them and at other times even defending them. (Rom. 2:14–15)

The apostle Paul emphasizes that all humans have a certain notion of the will of God. He intimates that this will can be "comprehended," grasped by the mind, through reflection. The common revelation of God in nature is therefore accessible, at least in part, to human reason, for it manifests itself in a certain moral sense. Paul goes a step farther, however, which grates on our modern ears: this partial revelation renders men and women "without excuse" (Rom 1:20 [Greek *anapologētous*]) since they have not given honor to the Creator. The fact that they do not acknowledge that God reveals himself through his work is to literally close their eyes, *deliberately* as it were: "Their thinking became futile and their foolish hearts were darkened" (Rom. 1:21); "They exchanged [*metallassō*] the truth about God for a lie" (Rom. 1:25); "They did not see fit [= they *refused*] to acknowledge God" (Rom. 1:28 RSV).

This pronouncement of Paul, founded on God's own pronouncement (indicated in the text by the word *wrath*), might appear harsh or excessive, if not unjust. While it is true that numerous phenomena of this world remain incomprehensible, such as evil and suffering in all their forms, they cannot be attributed to God because he is love and light (James 1:13; 1 John 1:5; 4:16).

Idolatry and the Reversal of the Creation Order

The revelation of God through nature establishes the responsibility of human beings in this world. It exposes, in a certain sense, their primordial "offense": "[They] served the creature rather than the Creator" (Rom. 1:25, RSV). In other words, they *worshiped* the creature; they *strove* after the creature alone.

The reversal is now complete: instead of exercising *dominion* over the fish, the birds, and reptiles—the species of every habitat— men and women have allowed creatures, whom they deify and worship, to have dominion over them; they *subject* themselves to them as they would idols. It should be noted here the "classification" system mentioned by Paul (birds, quadrupeds, reptiles) is nearly identical (with the exception of fish) to that of the book of Genesis (1:26, 28; 2:20; 7:14).

The law handed down by Moses to the people of Israel forbade the representation of God in the form of any creature or any object found "in heaven above or on the earth beneath or in the waters below" (Exod. 20:4). This particular injunction is completed by that against the worship of wood, stone, and metal graven images conceived by the imagination of man. Its basic purpose is to condemn the polytheistic cults of the ancient Middle East, which is also at the heart of the message proclaimed from the very first chapter of Genesis, in which the one God—Creator of the heavens, the lands and the seas, the animals and human beings—is distinct from his creation.

On the other hand, "animist" forms of worship, at first magic rites, are soon reinforced by various origin myths: the gods, to amuse themselves, beget men and women subject to their capricious desires during the course of sumptuous banquets, titanic combats, or dubious alliances; the world they created is thus tainted with "evil," contrary to the "good" (Heb. *tôv*: "good, nice, beautiful")—and even "exceedingly good"—creation, created by God "in the beginning" as stated in the Bible (Gen. 1:31).

Hundreds of deities have been inventoried in the Pantheon of ancient religions. Humans have been known to worship the gods of the cosmos (sun, moon, and stars), of the earth (springs, trees, wind, etc.), and the beasts of the field (ox, bull, serpent, birds, etc.). There are even gods with human faces, as images of virile strength or maternal fertility (i.e., Baal and Ashtoreth, who are mentioned in the Bible).

Man-God Master of the World

Some translators make a distinction between the material representation and the mental image, pointing out the difference in the Hebrew words *pesel* and *təmûnâh* in Exodus 20:4: "You shall not make for yourself a *carved image*, or any *likeness*" (ESV). The same distinction is sometimes drawn in Greek (see Rom. 1:23) between the terms *eikōn* ("identical image") and *homoiōma* ("abstract resemblance"). From the former derives the Greek word *eidōlon* ("idol")—the image of what one might *see* (as reflected in a mirror), were it an optical illusion. A pagan deity can thus come to personify a heightened human desire, such as the quests for increased fertility, power over the world, or even boundless riches. In a patently distorted way, man thereby puts himself in the place of the deity.

In condemning pagan idolatry, Paul begins by asserting that humans "exchanged the glory of the immortal God for images *resembling mortal man*" (Rom. 1:23; emphasis added). Of course, this charge concerns, in the first instance, those deities depicted with a human face or frame, such as the goddess Diana of Ephesus.

But mortal man can also mistake himself for the ultimate reference point and consider himself to be "godlike" (which is the primary temptation in the Garden of Eden). He believes he can discern on his own between good and evil, without having recourse to the transcendent God—the Lord of creation—who rules him. An inevitable chain reaction can often be observed: even when man believes himself emancipated from primitive idol worship, he invents for himself new idols, in his own image, so as to better render himself master of the universe.

Some have criticized the biblical view of "revelation," with its strong denunciation and condemnation of animistic and polytheistic forms of worship, for "desacralizing" nature, for emptying it of its "magical" power, and thus rendering it susceptible to the domination of man. But the awe inspired by natural phenomena is in reality driven by fear, which then becomes a source of superstition and withdrawal. Attempts are made to tame and pacify these formidable powers, if not to control them, by calling them by their "name."

The "fear of God" in the Bible is of an entirely different sort: it is tantamount to having a healthy *respect* for the Creator. It is also motivated by the deep-seated sentiment that springs from the commandment: "You shall *love* the Lord your God with all your heart and with all your soul and with all your might" (Deut. 6:5 ESV; emphasis added). Moreover, "There is no fear in love," as the apostle John writes (1 John 4:18). The fear of God thus consists in refraining from doing what displeases God, from breaking his commandments, from *transgressing* his laws, from leading life as if he didn't exist—in a word, from not recognizing that God alone is the Creator and Lord.

This is precisely what lies behind the biblical condemnation of animistic and polytheistic forms of worship, inasmuch as idolatrous practice leads directly to the disdaining, the diminishing, if not the undermining of creation altogether.

Limits and Transgression

The attitudes against which the apostle Paul inveighs throughout his letter to the Romans also tell a larger story: they reveal man's propensity for self-aggrandizement, for *overstepping the bounds* of his condition, as much in a spiritual as in moral and practical sense. Man's *unbridled* behavior has a negative impact on every sphere—be it familial, sexual, social, or economic—of human activity, hence the environment in the broadest sense, including what is termed "nature."

Paul begins by asserting that the judgment of God has been revealed against the "impiety" of human beings, which consists in their not maintaining a genuine and lovingly inspired personal relationship with the true God. This judgment is also directed against their "unrighteousness," which encompasses every kind of base behavior and, in particular, their penchant for "suppress[ing] the truth" (Rom. 1:18) or, more to the point, for "*exchang[ing]* the truth for a lie" (Rom.1:25). The end result is a kind of spiritual blindness, brought about both by their very enslavement to evil "desires" and by God himself, who thus renders his verdict against all unjust behavior.

The apostle Paul then goes on to discuss female and male homosexual practice, based on immoderate sexual desire and a *willful* change in behavior: women "*exchanged* [same verb as above] natural relations for unnatural ones," and men were "*inflamed with lust for one another*" (Rom. 1:26–27). This is an allusion to the frenzied and unbridled sexuality of the inhabitants of Sodom and Gomorrah in the Old Testament (Gen. 18–19).

But Paul denounces elsewhere, along with the other apostles, the other forms of sexual practice already condemned by the Law of Moses (Lev. 20:10–21); in particular, adultery, incest, and bestiality— hence every physical union outside of monogamous heterosexual marriage. This underscores the general human tendency to *transgress* the limits of the creation order, to twist or break the natural relationship between God and humans, then among humans themselves, and between humans and nature.

Broken Relationships and Pride

The prophets of the Old Testament and the apostles of the New (Jer. 31; Ezek. 16; Apoc. 21) often present the relationship between male and female as an image of the relationship between God and his people, united in reciprocal love. Every other extramarital relationship then becomes a metaphor for "spiritual adultery," for a "mixed" form of worship (polytheist and syncretistic) offered to idols, as opposed to worship of the one true God (Jer. 3:9; 5:7; 7:9; Ezek. 16:32; Rom. 2:22). Paul seems to suggest here that the more society moves away from the paradigm of the male-female couple, the less God's revealed image is perceived in the world.

This dislocation between human beings and their *environment* (in the broadest sense) ultimately manifests itself. Indeed, Paul does not limit himself to the condemnation of homosexual practice as a consequence of *spiritual* disorder, he adds immediately afterward some twenty terms (often overlooked!) that evoke the various *causes* of dysfunction, whether among individuals, in a couple, within a family, or in society at large—such as injustice, wickedness (or immorality, sexual abuse), greed, envy, wrath, strife, murder, deceit, lying, false witness, hatred of God, insolence, arrogance, violence, indifference to the suffering of others, disobedience of children toward their parents, foolish behavior, and so on.

Some commentators make a point here to establish a link with those lists compiled by the Stoic authors of old, who in turn inspired Jewish writers (most notably Philo of Alexandria): they inventory as many as 120 different terms! And it is no secret how attentive Greek writers were to condemn every form of *transgression* of limits—especially *pridefulness* (Gr. *hubris*)—which could jeopardize the stability of ancient society.

An Ever-Present Folly Today

In biblical thought, it is also through the respecting of limits established by God that humans are to find the alternative to unrestrained exploitation of creation and its deification (an idolatrous form of worship condemned by prophets and apostles alike). For in endeavoring to free themselves from God and in serving the creature rather than the Creator, Paul asserts that "claiming to be wise, they became fools" (Rom. 1:22).

In their own way, the secular "prophets" of our society make the same point today. In an editorial for the weekly magazine *Le Point*, Claude Imbert criticizes the roots of the world financial crisis in these terms:

The main culprit [of the financial crisis]—often forgotten—is pride. It is *hubris* which the ancient Greeks identified as the prime toxin of community life. Pride is the antithesis of "common sense," which is the layman's version of reason and experience. Many are those who are endowed with reason, very few have common sense. Common sense is not "trending" these days. It is absent from our temples of power and finance, snuffed out by the frenzies of the age, the giddiness of upward mobility, the escapism into the realms of virtual reality, the contempt for the golden mean, the disdain for moderation. . . . Common sense is in retreat before an entire unbridled generation of financial professionals, popinjays belonging to the caste of the Golden Calf.[2]

Philosopher Dominique Bourg authored a similar editorial in *L'Express* under the title "Learning to Live in a Finite World":

Our civilization has been built on the belief that finiteness can be surpassed, that the physical world can be mastered without limits, and in the myth of unending increase in riches. We are "ultramoderns," having for creed the continual pursuit of pleasure. [. . .] But we shall not be able to possess all we desire, for the unfettered freedom of modern society is no longer possible with 7 billion people on the planet, soon to be 9 billion. [. . .] We must stop thinking that material enrichment is an end in itself and return to a certain form of sobriety.[3]

The Environmental Crisis: Some Spiritual Roots

While it is thought-provoking to cite these insightful analyses of the negative impact of human behavior on society and the environment, the Bible underscores, however, that these problems have

---

[2] Claude Imbert, *Le Point* (October 9, 2008).
[3] Dominique Bourg, "Learning to Live in a Finite World," *L'Express* (September 24, 2009), 88–89.

profound spiritual roots. The severing of the relationship with God manifests itself in acts that have the human "heart" for a point of origin, since the heart is the seat of thought, reflection, desire, and emotion. In Mark 7:21–22, Jesus declares that "it is from within, out of a person's heart, that evil thoughts come—sexual immorality, theft, murder, adultery, greed, malice, deceit, lewdness, envy, slander, arrogance and folly."

Much has been made of the *physical* pollution of nature, while too often the spiritual and moral defilement at the root of all pollution is forgotten. The problem lies in the inner nature of human beings themselves, within their *hearts*, and not in the *surrounding* world. On the other hand, few are ever alarmed by the possible contamination of the heart through the ideas, images, and sounds of the ambient contemporary culture, especially with regard to young people, who are the most susceptible to mass media and social networking.

By rejecting God's common revelation in his creation, comprised of humankind and "nature" as a whole, men and women stress the creational bonds to their very breaking point, with all the nefarious consequences that entail, as much for themselves as for nature. They spurn their principal mission to exercise dominion over the earth in the respect of creation's right order: God is the Lord, the "first" in all things, for "The earth is the LORD's, and everything in it" (Ps. 24:1; cf. Ps. 50:12); men and women created in his image come second; they are to be stewards of his creation and subject to their Creator. When they usurp the place of God and overstep the limits of their "mission," they upset world order; they turn it "upside down," as the common expression so well puts it.

"Transhumanists" aim today at surpassing the biological limits of humans, whether physical or mental, employing the most sophisticated technologies, coupled with powerful software tools and "artificial intelligence." These "advances," applied most notably in the medical field, seek to prolong human life, indefinitely if possible, or at the very least to make it more bearable and content. Some would resort as well to the most powerful chemical means to achieve these ends or even look for a new living space on another planet for the new "posthumans"! This latter utopia seduces individuals ready to sacrifice everything and to spend fortunes in order to conquer this nonhuman and illusive "nowhere."[4]

Transhumanists claim to be concerned with ethics as well—though the effectiveness of their purported altruism is highly questionable when the temptation to become "like gods" (at least for certain individuals who have become "stronger," and who risk exercising a despotic dominance over those "weaker") has never been more pertinent since the very first days of creation. The danger is great that the divine order will be upset all the more by attempts to shape life as early as embryogenesis (with the attendant risks of eugenic blunders), in the image of the ideal human person. There is much more that could be said here about transhumanists who are tempted to thus "improve" their bodies, when humans nowadays actually move around less and less, using the natural resources of their own body, starting with their legs. Living within the real limits of the human body is without doubt better—certainly from an ecological point of view—than through the virtual world of false promises relative to posthuman self-glorification.

This is the reason why God gives his people a law that aims at setting limits and, in some measure, at reestablishing the creation order. God's law-giving also underscores the close relationship that exists between humans and creation, while rendering all due honor to the *Creator*.

---

[4] This is a reference to Sir Thomas More's coinage of the term "utopia," from the Greek *ou-topos*, meaning "no place" or "nowhere."—Trans.

3

THE LAWS AND LIMITS
OF HUMAN ACTIVITY

Do not make idols or set up an image or a sacred stone
for yourselves, and do not place a carved stone in your
land to bow down before it. I am the Lord your God.
Observe my Sabbaths and have reverence for my sanctuary. I am the Lord. If you follow my decrees and are
careful to obey my commands, I will send you rain in its
season, and the ground will yield its crops and the trees
their fruit. Your threshing will continue until grape harvest and the grape harvest will continue until planting,
and you will eat all the food you want and live in safety
in your land. I will grant peace in the land, and you will
lie down and no one will make you afraid. I will remove
wild beasts from the land, and the sword will not pass
through your country. . . . I will look on you with favor
and make you fruitful and increase your numbers, and
I will keep my covenant with you. You will still be eating last year's harvest when you will have to move it
out to make room for the new. I will put my dwelling
place among you. . . . But if you will not listen to me
and carry out all these commands, and if you reject my
decrees and abhor my laws and fail to carry out all my
commands and so violate my covenant, then I will do
this to you. . . . I will break down your stubborn pride
and make the sky above you like iron and the ground
beneath you like bronze. Your strength will be spent in
vain, because your soil will not yield its crops, nor will
the trees of your land yield their fruit. . . . I will turn
your cities into ruins and lay waste your sanctuaries. . . .

All the time that it lies desolate, the land will have the
rest it did not have during the sabbaths you lived in it.

(Lev. 26:1–35)

Human Beings in Relation to Nature

The laws of the Old Testament shed light on the relationship
between human beings, their faith in God, and nature. Indeed, in
the books of Leviticus (Lev. 26) and Deuteronomy (Deut. 28), in
particular in the formulation of blessings (promises) and curses
(warnings), a close link is drawn between obedience to the laws
handed down by Moses to the people of Israel and the enjoyment
of favorable climate conditions, soil fertility, and successful crop
growth. Finally, the worship rendered to God in love and grateful-
ness during the great agricultural festivals (Passover and Pentecost
in the spring, the Feast of Tabernacles or *Sukkot* in the fall) is the
logical consequence of a life of obedience. The prophets establish
the same link between obedience to God and a favorable environment, and the reverse: If the natural environment is disturbed, it
is first of all the fault of the people of God who go astray on the
religious level by indulging in polytheistic cults dominated by "the
Baal and the Ashtars" (see, for example, Hos. 2 and 4).

All creation is therefore interdependent. In principle, human
beings—by their trust (i.e., faith) in God and their proper conduct both toward God (i.e., through obedience to the law) and
toward humanity (i.e., through their righteous dealings with one
another)—can cultivate and maintain the resources entrusted to
them. As prudent and wise managers, they can ensure the safeguard
and welfare of the entire creation. This attitude expresses itself, in
the first instance, in love of God alone and the rejection of idolatry
(Deut. 6:4), and in Sabbath-keeping and neighborly love (Lev. 19:6).

This attitude remains an ideal to strive for. Ever since the "fall,"
when the covenant with God was broken, the world has been
tainted by the presence of evil. It would then be a stretch, to say the
least, to consider every current woe in the world, every individual

or collective suffering, to be a consequence of specific trespasses against God. Alas, we know all too well what abuses this simplistic interpretation can lead to.

All of creation, as the apostle Paul makes clear, is subject to a "bondage of decay" (Rom. 8:21), for the earth and its inhabitants are "under the power of sin" (Rom. 3:9). But we are also told by the apostle that Jesus himself became "a curse for us" (Gal. 3:13). The Son of God took on himself the curse that weighs on humanity and affects the entire creation, enduring suffering and death for the salvation of both humanity and nature; but he also rose from the grave to bear witness to his victory over sin and death in order to make the blessing open to all.

God can thus reveal his presence to men and women, or he can cause them to sense his distance and hence disapproval, whether in the most pleasant times or in the most somber. In Matthew 5:45, Jesus expresses this truth in a vivid metaphor: "He causes his sun to rise on the evil and the good, and sends rain on the righteous and the unrighteous."

Human Beings Overstepping their Bounds

It nevertheless remains true that if men and women were to yield themselves as much as possible to the right creation order, if they were to respect the "priorities" laid down for their own good by the Creator, if they were to worship God in love and gratitude, then the earth and all who inhabit it and all that it contains would be far better off.

If man were obedient to his God, he would be the means of blessing for the earth. But in his insatiable greed, his contempt for creational equilibrium, his short-sighted selfishness, he contaminates it, he destroys it, he turns the garden into a desert.[1]

---

[1] Blocher, *In the Beginning*, 181.

"Sin" has been defined as the failure humanity to fully attain the "mark"—the ideal of the law laid down by God through Moses. But this fact does not exempt us from striving toward that goal, which is summed up in the injunction to love both God and neighbor. Under these circumstances, only faith in God can help men and women resolve this wrenching conflict, whose consequences reverberate as much in society as in nature. For passionate desires often hold sway over reason, deep-seated dissatisfaction often overwhelms personal contentment, and covetousness often exacerbates the drive to possess with any kind of restraint, so that men and women crave for themselves what belongs to others. These "passions" cancel out the very best humanistic aspirations to "do good." The apostle Paul expresses this dilemma in tragic terms: "For I have the desire to do what is good, but I cannot carry it out. For I do not do the good I want to do, but the evil I do not want to do—this I keep on doing" (Rom. 7:18–19).

The Relationship between Time and Money

"Time is money!" The catchphrase of modern humanity has become the source of tensions and tumult in every corner of the globe. It is normal to observe a chain of causes and effects in nature that is then up to humans to endeavor to understand so as to control them. By doing this, they could gain a certain advantage in order to adapt better to the world and live more comfortably. This is the point of science.

Yet if this approach to the world remains purely mechanistic, if resources are consumed without taking God into consideration, without yielding to the divine order, without well-defined ethical rules, without *limits*, then the danger of mismanaging and destroying creation becomes all the greater. Indeed, the desire to control nature in order to derive the maximum and the most immediate profit—which is motivated by *greed* or the love of money, which becomes a merciless god—leads men and women to challenge the notions of time, space, and nature as a whole.

Jesus explained to his followers, "You cannot serve both God and money," evoking Mammon, the personified idol of riches. In his letters, Paul also condemns greed on several occasions, which he likewise categorizes as "idolatry" (Col. 3:5). This goes to the heart of the spiritual problem, which leads humanity to reverse the creation order. They overstep their bounds in order to satisfy their most foolhardy desires. Their insatiable greed hinders them from considering what is right or wrong—which has an obvious impact on the environment.

Overuse and Overconsumption

An ethos driven by the desire to make a fast dollar and lead a lavish lifestyle manifests itself, most notably, in the overuse of natural resources and the overconsumption of goods produced in manufacturing. This in turn engenders pollution, societal disintegration, and poverty—problems that are everywhere decried and in evidence today.

Science has developed to the point where it can modify the inner structures of matter or living things in their genetic make-up, though it does not always take into account the repercussions. In several fields of applied research, scientists are playing the sorcerer's apprentice. In France, as in several other countries, "regulated research" on stem cells taken from human embryos has been authorized, in principle exclusively for medical purposes (this legislation was adopted by Parliament on July 16, 2013, with no real public debate). This legal maneuvering undermines, however, the Civil Code's call for "the respect for human life from conception" (Article 16). Genetic tinkering, such as human cloning, should be the subject of strict oversight, as this could well cross a frightening boundary for the human race. But how should lawmakers set these limits in the future? Should research laboratories take the lead?[2]

---

[2] On the research to improve the DNA of human embryos, see for example the article by Steve Connor concerning the work of Shoukhrat

The word *transgression* has never been more pertinent than it is in societies today. There could be well-founded questions concerning practices that are neither necessary nor indispensable, although they may be technically possible. For example, should a form of eugenics be tolerated on the grounds that a simple blood analysis of an expectant mother during the first trimester of pregnancy serves to collect information on the embryo, such as the sex of the future child or its potential debilitating illnesses? What should be the decision of parents in some Western countries where abortion is permitted up until the twelfth week of pregnancy?

Other examples of "transgression" could be cited here that raise, to say the least, ethical issues. Today, human genes can be inserted into the genome of animals for therapeutic purposes (such as insulin obtained by inserting a human gene into the genome of a bovine). The barrier between species has been crossed in a number of ways. At times veritable sessions of "genetic cuisine" take place in research laboratories where whatever strikes the fancy is thrown into the mix. To prove the point, it suffices to consult the scientific literature.

Transgenic Organisms

What should be thought then of the much-publicized GMOs (genetically modified organisms)? It is understandable that scientists should seek to improve the "natural" characteristics of a given species through the introduction of a gene from a different variety of the same species. This "artificial selection" completes and re-

---

Mitalipov, researcher at the Oregon Health and Science University, "Rewriting Life First Human Embryos Edited in U.S.," *MIT Technological Review* (July 26, 2017). See also the article by Yann Verdo, "Quelles limites aux manipulations génétiques," published in *Les Echos* (February 27, 2017), in which the author mentions the American and French legislation on the subject, notably the use of "molecular scissors" to modify the genome of the human embryo.

places the "empirical selection" that has been practiced for millennia in animal husbandry and agriculture.

It might be argued that GMO plant production offers increased safety (and therefore less uncertainty) for the farmer and that it reduces pollutants in some cases (for example, in pest control) and perhaps production costs (which remains to be proven). It is also possible on the other hand that this "improvement" serves only to reinforce intensive monocultures, whose negative effects are now known both in terms of biodiversity and the healthy equilibrium of these specific cultures.

In cases where a planted crop is rendered resistant to a weed killer sold by the same manufacturer that offers the genetically modified seed, it is reasonable to ask on purely "ecological" grounds: Should the genetic structure of a plant be modified *so that* more (or at least as much) herbicide might be spread? Or might it be better instead to seek to reduce the usage of pesticides, if not to do away with them entirely? And what should become of "wild" transgenic species modified through spontaneous hybridization in nature?

A more controversial threshold is crossed when a modified plant becomes the patented property of the inventor, which is most often the case. It then becomes impossible for the farmer to save seed from his crop (since it is "programed" to expire). He is obligated to buy each year the same genetically modified seed. If the seed market does not pose too much of a problem in developed countries (as it is a common practice), then it turns into a major obstacle in the poorest nations where people find themselves enslaved to a system ill-adapted to their often-precarious situation. Lastly, it is legitimate to question whether it is right to "patent life forms" (genetically modified animals, for example, or medicinal plants recently discovered) for purely commercial reasons.

There are no easy answers to these questions, nor moreover to that of establishing limits for scientific research, and yet the examples of biological transgression are endless and sometimes worrisome. Just how far will human beings go to "master" nature and "submit" it to their will?

Lust for Power and Destruction of Nature

This manner of treating and exploiting nature, driven essentially by an overweening desire for control, results in increased pollution of the earth, oceans, and living organisms—sometimes in an irreversible way, at least in terms of short or midterm solutions. The ecological tragedies that shook the 1970s to the 1990s, such as oil spills and lethal contaminations, thus gave rise to great waves of protest against the excesses of industrial society.

It will suffice to cite here a triad of disasters that haunt the collective memory: Seveso (Italy, 1976), Bhopal (India, 1984), Chernobyl (USSR-Ukraine, 1986). Nor can be forgotten the first oil spill in Torrey Canyon in 1967 and those that followed at the rate of one major accident every ten years: Amoco-Cadiz (1978), Exxon Valdez (1989), Erika (1999), Prestige (2002), BP's oil rig Deepwater Horizon (2010), and so on.

Sometimes natural disasters occur simultaneously with an industrial accident, such as Fukushima in March 2011 on the Japanese coast where a strong earthquake (magnitude 9 on the Richter scale) caused a powerful tsunami, which itself partially destroyed a nuclear power plant. The full consequences of this accident are still poorly understood, both in Japan and along faraway foreign coasts impacted by radioactive waste carried by ocean currents. Oil pollution due to armed conflicts should also be taken into account, as for example during the Gulf War in 1991 when very large quantities of oil were set on fire and spilled on the ground and in the sea. Generally speaking, conflicts always result in the destruction of natural habitats and major pollution, the extent of which may vary according to the type of weapons used (chemical, bacteriological, nuclear, etc.).

Hazardous conditions due to chemicals continue to increase in the world. Several thousand new products, whether natural or synthetic, are indexed *each day* in the *Chemical Abstracts* registry. Over 140 million organic and inorganic substances have been identified, and yet it seems as though only about 3% have been subjected to a peer-reviewed toxicological study.[3]

The United Nations Environment Programme (UNEP), in cooperation with the World Health Organization (WHO), has been overseeing the implementation of a strategic approach to reduce the effects of the most damaging chemical substances for human health. Among the most hazardous are asbestos, arsenic, benzene, cadmium, dioxins (including the infamous polychlorinated biphenyls or PCBs), mercury, lead, and various pesticides. Prolonged exposure to these products—especially during mining, production, transport, and basic use (including regular consumption via vegetable and animal products) and disposal—is considered carcinogenic.

It has come to the point where strenuous criticism is being leveled today at the consequences of the prodigious amount of plastic produced and dispersed in the world, polluting for an alarming period of time our lands, clogging up numerous rivers in developing countries, and forming veritable "continents" in our oceans. Furthermore, it is known that plastic materials decompose into very fine particles that can be ingested by land and sea animals or seep into the ground as deep as water tables. Current legislation is gradually banning "single-use" plastic (e.g., plates, plastic ware, and straws) as a first step toward tighter control over the production of this highly valued and controversial material, which will in any case eventually be designed to be fully recyclable. Outer space itself is polluted by the debris of some 5,000 rockets and satellites launched since 1957. Over 20,000 objects of varying size now gravitate in orbit around our planet, most at an altitude of between 800 and 2,000 kilometers, which multiplies when they collide with one another.

---

[3] In other words, about 4 million, though the figure is difficult to ascertain and verify. See on this subject www.prc.cnrs-gif.fr, and most notably the list of carcinogenic agents at http://www.prc.cnrs.fr/IMG/pdf/agents-cancerogenes-circ-v22022016-2.pdf and www.saicm.org.

Pollution on a worldwide scale provokes justified reactions. Although measures to reduce this pollution are now beginning to have some effect, they remain far from sufficient.

Materialist and Religious Critiques

Since the nineteenth century, scientific literature has drawn a vivid sketch of the disastrous effects produced by humankind's blind dominion over nature. It was the French naturalist Jean-Baptiste de Lamarck (1744–1829) who underscored this very point from a materialistic and atheistic perspective in his definition of "man" in an encyclopedia entry:

> Man, by his self-centeredness too short-sighted for his own best interest, by his inclination to luxuriate in every pleasure within reach, in a word, by his total lack of concern for the future and for other human beings, seems to work for the annihilation of his very means of conservation as well as for the destruction of his own species. In everywhere laying waste to the large plants that protect the soil, in exchange for goods that satisfy his passing greediness, man soon brings about the infertility of the land which he inhabits, causes springs to dry up, and drives away animals that once found therein their sustenance. He causes large swaths of the earth that were formerly fertile and heavily populated to become barren, unproductive, uninhabitable, and deserted.[4]

A more recent reprise of this "definition" has been articulated by Pope John Paul II in an encyclical letter (*Centesimus annus*, 1991), almost in the same terms (intentionally), but this time with a pronounced spiritual application:

---

[4] Jean-Baptiste de Lamarck, *Nouveau dictionnaire d'histoire naturelle, appliquée aux arts, à l'agriculture, à l'économie rurale et domestique, à la médecine, etc.*, vol. 15 (Paris: Deterville, 1817), 270–71.

In his desire to accumulate and revel in rather than to be and grow, man consumes the resources of the earth and his very life in an excessive and disordered way. At the root of this senseless destruction of the natural environment lies an anthropological error, which unfortunately is widespread in our day. . . . Man thinks that he can make arbitrary use of the earth, subjecting it without restraint to his will, as if the earth did not have its own design and prior God-given purpose, which man can indeed develop but must not betray. Instead of fulfilling his role as co-operator with God in the work of creation, man sets himself up in place of God and only ends up provoking a rebellion on the part of nature, which is more tyrannized by him than governed.

Profit in itself is a legitimate pursuit, but not without limits. The same goes for economic growth, which reflects a changing world whose development might be considered positive, but it is not right for economic growth to control mind-sets and influence behaviors—to the point where it imposes on human beings a form of bondage.

A Market Gone Haywire

Economic growth today has become a veritable obsession of humanity. The analysts of the global market issue their daily prognostications, which buyers and sellers spin to their own personal ends, often twisted by greed.

The merits of free exchange for the greater common good cannot be questioned; however, there is no denying on that account the reality of the passions that drive the various actors of the market—sellers, buyers, and consumers. All end up dependent, to the very point of bondage, on the whims of this truly intrusive and overbearing "Leviathan." Just as in the book of Revelation, this one-world economic Babylon can come crashing down "in a single hour," to the great dismay of humankind and especially the financial sector. The long litany of traded goods in that doomsday scenario includes human trafficking, which is mentioned last behind metals, textiles, lumber, and rare spices (Rev. 18:10–13). Some commentators do not hesitate to interpret the reference to "slaves" (literally, "bodies and souls of men," YLT) as those lives that have been shattered by overwork and overeager economic activity. In this same book, a stern warning is issued against "those who destroy [morally and physically] the earth" (Rev. 11:18).

Several biblical injunctions run counter to the narrow notion of "cost effectiveness" based on self-serving gain. For example, the owner of a wheat field, olive grove, or grapevine is forbidden from returning to reap or harvest whatever is left after a first pass, so as to leave it for the widow, the orphan, and the foreigner, who are then permitted to glean their own crop to feed themselves (Deut. 24:19–22); and the ox must not be muzzled when it is treading out the grain and prevented from having its share (Deut. 25:4).

Contentment: Between Reason and Faith

Beyond the driving and measurable forces of the economy, which can be described and analyzed in a scientific and rigorous way, the most unexpected, the most irrational human behaviors must be taken into account without overlooking their spiritual dimension. The lust for riches, among other ambitions, goads humanity into subjugating creation to the despotic demands of an ever-increasing yield or profit margin, beyond what is necessary and reasonable.

At the same time, it is a lack of trust, of "faith" if one wills, that leads men and women in "developed" societies to surround themselves with safety measures, the most comprehensive insurance policies, the most ironclad laws, to a point where society as a whole becomes paralyzed. They are incapable of undertaking endeavors with restraint and wisdom, of striking a balance between freedom and responsibility.

In order to lay hold of healthy growth, we must learn to be patient and "content"; that is, satisfied with what we already have, rather than frustrated with what we do not yet possess. This assumes that we seek justice, in particular for the poor, and that we curb the overexploitation of creation. This will doubtless require a return to a simpler mode of existence:

> The Bible reminds us that, for an ancient Hebrew man, happiness consisted in being able to repose in his own vineyard, under a fig tree—both symbols of prosperity and security—for, in his garden retreat, he was light-years away from the thousand and one temptations of modern life.[5]

Resting trustfully in God is probably one of the surest means of working for justice and avoiding the premature depletion of natural resources of the planet, if not their complete ruin.

A Biblical Safeguard: The Sabbath

> Remember the Sabbath day by keeping it holy. Six days you shall labor and do all your work, but the seventh day is a sabbath to the LORD your God. On it you shall not do any work, neither you, nor your son or daughter, nor your male or female servant, nor your animals, nor any foreigner residing in your towns. For in six days the LORD made the heavens and the earth, the sea, and all that is in them, but he rested on the seventh day. Therefore the LORD blessed the Sabbath day and made it holy.
> (Exod. 20:8–11)

The Sabbath was established following the biblical narrative of creation in "seven days." The people of Israel therefore had to observe the Sabbath and could not work the seventh day of the week. This was a rather radical novelty in the ancient Middle East, for the Sabbath affected every man and woman of society, including "slaves" and foreigners. Every individual had the right to a weekly rest.

The Sabbath was one of the limits imposed by God on his people, a safeguard to prevent them from breaking the creational

---

[5] Jean-Marie Pelt, *La terre en héritage* (Paris: Fayard, 2000), 257.

bonds. By observing this day set apart, in thanksgiving and reverence for the Lord of creation, man comes to understand that he is
a created being bound by time and space and that he cannot live
in a completely autonomous manner, nor count exclusively on his
own strength or labor to satisfy his needs. This was a practical way
of cautioning the people of Israel against the temptation to deify
nature or living things. The Sabbath appears, then, as a reminder
of the creation order.

Finally, the Sabbath is a day that celebrates the Liberator God,
in which there is rejoicing for the deliverance from bondage in
Egypt (Deut. 5:15). The Sabbath is a tangible sign of the exclusive relationship that exists between God and his people (Exod. 31:12–17).
It should be noted that the order to observe the Sabbath is sometimes juxtaposed with that of rejecting all idolatry (Exod. 23:12–13).

The Sabbath of the Land

Working animals have a right to a Sabbath's rest and the land
shall "enjoy its sabbaths," resting every seven years in order to be
more fertile (Lev. 25:2; 26:34, 43). God then promises his people a
bumper crop, a harvest nothing short of miraculous, in the sixth
year in order to be able to spend the sabbatical year (and thus the
year thereafter until the new harvest) in the best possible conditions,
without suffering want (Lev. 25:18–22). On the other hand, when
the commandments of the Mosaic Law are transgressed, in particular the law of the Sabbath, the land will "vomit out" its inhabitants;
the people will then be subjected to the harsh laws of voluntary or
forced exile (Lev. 18:25, 28; 20:22).

This biblical imagery speaks volumes. The land *rejoices* to be at
rest when the people of Israel show themselves faithful to God, but
it recoils from overuse and endures the consequences of the religious unfaithfulness of humans, becoming sick to the point of *vom-
iting*. A Solomonic proverb vividly expresses the consequences of a
proneness to gluttony: "If you have found honey, eat only enough
for you, lest you have your fill of it and vomit it" (Prov. 25:16 ESV).

Rest and Faith

Rest is linked to the grace of God, to his love. It's a sign of the dependence of human beings on the Lord, of their trust in the One who provides generously for their needs, even when they rest. There is no real rest without faith in God. A good many businesspersons, industry leaders, artisans, lawyers, doctors, and so on could learn from this truth in order to avoid falling into a bondage that ruins their family life and health, which in the final analysis undermines their efficiency and the quality of their work, not to mention the negative consequences it has on the environment. It is indeed dangerous to turn work into a new idol.

Men and women may have dominion over creation on the condition that they themselves remain submitted to God by putting his commandments into practice. By observing the Sabbath, in particular, God invites them to rest and trust. The author of the letter to the Hebrews underscores this point in a new perspective: It is in this way that God promises freedom to his people and that the Sabbath—the symbol par excellence of spiritual rest—finds its full meaning, which is freedom regained to live in communion with God and to strive toward the ideal of his law. Faith and rest are thus linked, so that the land and the human beings who cultivate and inhabit it might prosper all the more.

Is it therefore necessary to strictly keep the Sabbath? Observing a day of rest devoted to God and to contribute to the well-being of those around us is a healthy practice, on the condition that the Sabbath does not become another means of shackling human persons to an inescapable ritualistic obligation. The Sabbath is made for man, Jesus reminds us, and not the other way around (Mark 2:27). However, there is no true freedom without exercising a genuine sense of responsibility. This is the price to be paid in order to take care of what God has created. All is grace. The gospel gives fresh meaning to that memorable phrase.

4

THE GOSPEL AND PROTECTION OF THE ENVIRONMENT

The connection between the gospel and creation care is not obvious *a priori*. What is the association, in effect, between the advent of Jesus Christ in the world—his life, teaching, death on a Roman cross, resurrection, "sacrifice" for the salvation of humanity—and the protection of the environment as it is defined today?

Ecology and History

The question of creation care did not present itself in similar terms two millennia ago. At the time of Jesus, the effects of human activity on the world were not as harmful for the environment as they are today. One cannot compare our industrialized societies over the past two centuries, in Europe and in North America, with the agrarian societies of the ancient Middle East or the Greek and Roman Empires. On the other hand, it would be incorrect to maintain that these civilizations have nothing in common, at least in terms of their relationship to creation. For it would be erroneous to assume that the watershed moment introduced by the life, death, and resurrection of Jesus Christ changed nothing in ancient times and that it remains without effect in our day. It would be likewise misguided to assume that our contemporaries have nothing to learn from biblical teaching.

The situations are analogous and share some key points—namely, the continuance of the "cultural mandate" since the creation of the world, as well as that of the "missionary mandate" associated with the gospel of Jesus Christ. Both have a direct impact on the relationship of human beings to creation. The specific biblical injunctions of Genesis may have not come directly down to all the peoples of the Mediterranean basin or the ancient Middle East; they are not a common reference point for all of our contemporaries. But their universal and permanent character remains within the framework of general revelation.

In antiquity, people groups from every nation were already acutely aware of the need to take care of the earth, as agriculture was the dominant field of work in ancient societies. Now, we know that "ecological" problems were already present in ancient times. Overgrazing in the Mediterranean countries, for example, considerably depleted the soils. We can still see traces of it in the landscape.

A Long-Established Policy and Practice

It will undoubtedly be objected that the ancients were unaware of these harmful farming practices. This would be to ignore, then, the writings of antiquity's great "agronomists," such as the twenty-eight volumes on Carthaginian agriculture (presently in the region now occupied by Tunisia), composed in the Punic language by Magon (or Mago) at the turn of the third to second century BC. This treatise was translated into Latin after the seizure of Carthage (146 BC) by the order of the Roman Senate. It then enjoyed a wide dissemination throughout the empire.

This would be to disregard as well Virgil (70–19 BC), who himself participated in the redevelopment of lands left neglected by veterans who had inherited them after the war between Anthony and Octavius. The Latin poet provides invaluable information—in verse, no less!—concerning the restoration and the cultivation of soils in Campania and Latium. It is worth consulting Virgil's *Georgics*, for example, where he "hymns" the virtues of crop rotation so as to foster the "work" of the earth (Book I). Lastly, Columella's *De Rusticae* in particular should be mentioned here, for he inventoried as early as the first century all the known treatises of his agronomist predecessors in the Latin world.

This would be to also disregard the remarkable work of the agronomist Qûtâmä in the third century AD. His *Book of Nabatean Agriculture* is a veritable and thoroughgoing agronomic treatise, inspired by ancient Mesopotamian tradition. It describes the most appropriate farming practices for Babylonian lands, often the most sophisticated techniques of the era, especially for the preservation, amendment, and restoration of soils. It analyzes with razor sharpness economic questions relative to agriculture, land ownership, the ideal farm size, the various kinds of crops (sometimes mixed), and yields. Finally, it adds to the mix more spiritual considerations, albeit against a theosophical or esoteric backdrop in a polytheistic context, concerning the moral and religious attitudes of farmers in their capacity as owners of agricultural lands. It signals out for condemnation, most notably, greed and every form of over-cultivation and poor management of the land.[1]

Each one of these treatises mentions the need to care for the earth, and especially to restore it if damaged as a result of neglect or poor treatment. This suggests that a form of "environmental protection," considered indispensable for ensuring the survival of populations, was already in place in antiquity.

Problems arise today, almost in the same terms, in the rural societies of developing countries. This is particularly the case in Sub-Saharan Africa, where the measures implemented to protect the environment are all the more critical in that they are mostly directed at the agricultural sector and thus help to ensure the feeding of communities. In Europe, it is the abandonment of agricultural land that is of concern. In France, over the course of the twentieth century, the number of farmers has diminished tenfold, most often with almost general indifference to their great despair. The same observation can be made in a fair number of other European countries where this "desertion" has a real impact on the

---

[1] See the remarkable analysis of this work by Mohammed El Faïz, *L'agronomie de la Mésopotamie antique* (Leiden: Brill, 1995).

environment—although it might not always be negative one, for example, if proper reforestation is monitored. Among the factors explaining the neglect that results in ecological harm, the religious dimension is often ignored, which plays a clear role since it is intimately linked to the daily lives of populations.

The Gospel and its Positive Effects

The gospel profoundly renewed the mentalities of men and women living the first century and still does today, due to all the positive results that can be expected from a proper management of the earth and its resources.

In the first chapter of the Epistle to the Romans, the apostle Paul proclaims: "For I am not ashamed of the gospel, because it is the power of God that brings salvation to everyone who believes: first to the Jew, then to the Gentile" (v. 16). This statement precedes his taking up the theme of God's revelation through creation, which concerns all peoples—Jews and non-Jews.

In the context of the covenant made by God with Moses and his people, the Jews had the benefit of a particular revelation from God. As Paul demonstrates in Roman 3–8, this "special" revelation, introduced by the first covenant between God and Israel, has henceforth been extended through Jesus, the Messiah (or the Christ[2]), as part of the "new covenant" to include all humanity, as much for the Jews as for the Gentiles.

The Law of Moses reveals the holy will of God, which is reflected in love put into practice (Deut. 6:5; Lev. 19:18; Matt. 22:36–40), and it establishes a certain world order over which God reigns

---

[2] The terms "Messiah" and "Christ" are synonymous; the former derives from Hebrew (*mashiach*), the latter from Greek (*Christos*). Both may be translated as "the anointed one," which refers to the anointing with oil practiced by the ancient Hebrews to dedicate a priest, king, or prophet to the service of God. Jesus carries out these three functions and is thus "the Anointed One" par excellence.

as Lord. Human beings are incapable of fulfilling this law, based in perfect love, to its complete extent and requirements (Deut. 30–31; Ps. 14:2). God's forgiveness is nevertheless open to anyone who acknowledges their "shortcomings," their utter inability to love God and neighbors as they should, so as to be reckoned "righteous." Thus, to those who sincerely desire to turn away from the "evil" that presses in on them and to live by doing good, the grace of God is abundantly offered. This was first made possible under the old covenant (Lev. 17:11) through the sacrifice of an animal whose blood "covers/erases" the offense; but now all the more so in Jesus, the Son of God who became incarnate in this world to inaugurate the new covenant "by his blood" (Luke 22:20), as had long been announced by the prophets (Isa. 53; Jer. 31:31–34).

The gospel can be summed up as follows: through his death, Jesus *covers and erases* trespasses or "sins" with respect to the law (expiation); his life is given *in the place* of the guilty (substitution); and it is offered as a ransom *to redeem* human beings, to pay their "debt" before God (redemption). By his resurrection, the Lamb of God (John 1:29; Rev. 5:6) and the Great High Priest (Heb. 4:14) has become the "mediator of a new covenant," complete and final, between God and his people; he makes righteous before the Supreme Judge, forever, whoever simply puts their faith, their trust, in him. It is thus truly "good news" for every human being.

Lastly, by his death and resurrection, Jesus paved the way for the reconciliation of the "cosmos" (the world in the broadest sense) with God. Indeed, the universe created by God benefits from the effects of this great redemption wrought by the Messiah/Christ. This is the conclusion of the apostle Paul in chapter 8, which closes his "theological treatise" on law, judgment, and grace in his Epistle to the Romans (see also Col. 1:20).

A New Relationship with the Environment

A life-giving relationship is reestablished between the "head"—Jesus, the Son of God—and the members of his "body," which are all those who believe in him, Jews and non-Jews alike. God grants them his Spirit, so they can recognize him as their Father and receive the strength to fulfill the law through love. From thence comes their new relationship with the world that surrounds them—that is, with their environment.

This makes it easier to understand why Paul is not ashamed to consider the gospel, the good news of the love of God manifested in Christ crucified and resurrected, as a powerful agent offered for the salvation of humankind and for the redemption of the entire creation. The right order of creation begins to reestablish itself when human beings worship God who is "above all," the veritable "center" toward which all things converge, the *Lord* to whom belongs the earth and all that it contains. Human beings can then enjoy renewed and transformed relationships, and be more in harmony with the creation order, with their neighbors, and with their environment.

The gospel has then a very tangible impact. Reconciliation with God leads to even greater respect for fellow human beings created in the divine image and to seeking their welfare and prosperity. This includes care for creation and the sharing of resources dedicated to the sound management of society. In other words, the ideal of the Mosaic Law is superseded by that of the "anthem to love," such as Jesus expresses to his apostles the night before his death (John 13–17). In 1 Corinthians 13, Paul later becomes love's most eloquent bard.

There is thus an intimate link between the gospel—faith in Jesus Christ, the Savior and Lord of the earth—and the protection of the environment. Putting this notion into practice, however, will prove to be more difficult.

Christians and the Ecological Crisis

In a 1967 article in the journal *Science*, American historian Lynn White Jr. (son of a liberal Presbyterian theologian and professor of ethics of the same name) asserts and attempts to show that Christians bear a particular responsibility for the ecological crisis. His criticism falls mainly on the *anthropocentrism* Christian religion has promoted—namely, its view of the "central" position of humanity in the world as the be-all and end-all of everything, which grants humanity the intellectual and practical preeminence to dominate the entire world—alas, often at the expense of nature.[3]

During the same period, writers such as Jean Dorst, professor at the National Museum of Natural History in Paris, not only seconded this critique of Christianity, but pointed out its Greek and Latin philosophical roots:

> It is legitimate to draw a contrast between Eastern philosophies and our Western notions. Many East Asians have in effect a respect for life in all its forms, all proceeding directly from God or even being considered a part of him, thus man belongs mystically to a complex of which he represents but one element.

> In contrast, Western philosophies all stress the supremacy of man over the rest of creation, which, in return, only exist to serve as background scenery. These statements, made by the pagan philosophers of Antiquity, provide the foundation for Christian teaching.[4]

Dorst cites in support of his claim the biblical command to subdue the earth (Gen. 1:28–29) and elaborates thus:

> [These statements] were taken up by the mass of philosophers in the Western system of thought, including the most materialist among them, all esteeming man to be the supreme creature to whom everything must submit itself. It is hardly surprising

---

[3] In response to this article, it will be of interest to read the open letter by Jacques Arnould, "Les racines historiques de notre crise écologique. Lettre à Lynn White et à ceux qui s'en réclament," *Pardès*, no. 39 (February 2005), 211–19.

[4] Jean Dorst, *Avant que nature meure. Pour une écologie politique* (Neuchâtel: Delachaux et Niestlé, 1965; 6th ed., revised and enlarged, 1978), 26–27.

then that the protection of animals and plants was given short shrift by European philosophy from which our technical civilization directly derives.[5]

It might be objected here that Christian theologians did not "base" their teaching on Greek philosophy (on Plato and Aristotle in particular), and that, in any case, they approached this tradition through the prism of biblical revelation. But it is also true that they borrowed this philosophical "framework" (mainly Aristotelian) for convenience, often for lack of a better "scientific" understanding in the modern sense of the word. Lastly, it is true that man and woman appear as the crowning glory of the creation work of God, that they are called to have dominion over and subdue creation, yet not of course as its center and end. Their earthbound status remains under the rule of God, and they may not manage creation through the exercise of independent reason alone.[6]

A Rational Dominion

It would be worthwhile in this light to examine the work of Francis Bacon (1560–1626)—namely, *The New Atlantis* (and most pertinently, the *desiderata* indicated in the list of *Magnalia Naturae*, often appended to this text). In this book, Bacon justifies without apology the dominion of man over nature, and he introduces a secularizing component into this dynamic: that is, the marvelous works of creation are now attributed to *Nature* and no longer to *God* as in traditional theology.

Nevertheless, his is more the Cartesian "I" of "I think, therefore I am"—man availing himself of his reason alone as a guide—which

---

[5] Ibid.

[6] On this point, see Samuel Bénétreau, "Critique de la thèse d'un anthropocentrisme biblique écologiquement ravageur," *Théologie Evangélique* 15, no. 3 (2016): 51–80. See as well the encyclical letter of Pope Francis, *Laudato Si'* (Paris: Parole et Silence, 2015), 90–101.

will provide the impetus to a modern notion of dominion over nature, all too soon disassociated from its biblical and Christian roots.

In his *Discourse on the Method*, Descartes (1596–1650) asserts that the general notions he has acquired (and holds for certain) in the field of physics allow him—nay, even oblige him—"to do all that is possible for the general welfare of mankind." Descartes explains that by "recognizing the power and the effects of fire, water, air, the stars, the heavens and all the other bodies in our environment, as clearly as we know the various crafts of our artisans, we could put these bodies to use in all the appropriate ways and thus render ourselves the masters and keepers of Nature."[7]

In the Part Six of his *Discourse*, Descartes adds, with a praiseworthy altruistic concern, that this "dominion" must in the first instance find its application in the field of medicine. For mastering nature should not be a matter of satisfying the desire alone to invent for ourselves "untold numbers of devices that would give us the carefree enjoyment of the fruits of the earth and of all the goods we find therein, principally with a view towards the preservation of health."[8] Apparently, a sound body favors thought and action, especially for the exploitation of the earth's resources for human advantage!

For the most part, it is this Cartesian heritage of modern science that Dorst contests. He condemns its impact on nature, though he concludes in a more positive manner:

> Whatever may be our personal ideological opinions, they will have little bearing on the solution to the problem we face. For even if man had the moral right to subjugate the world for his own benefit alone, he can only do so in the most optimal way, for biologists are agreed that this is only possible if he yields himself to certain natural laws and by respecting an equilibrium he cannot modify beyond a certain point.[9]

---

[7] René Descartes, *Discourse on the Method*, 4th ed. (New York: Hackett, 1999).

[8] Ibid.

[9] Dorst, *Avant que nature meure*, 27.

Christianity and Ecology

Although it relies in part on false premises, the charge of anthropocentrism leveled by Lynn White deserves to be taken seriously. It is undeniable that Christian civilization has not always been a stellar model, either individually or collectively, of good management of natural resources. On that score, White can be credited with being among the first in his time to draw attention to the ecological cause in the United States.

It should be added here that the qualifier "Christian" or the concept of "Christian civilization" are perhaps not the most appropriate. First in Europe and later in America, it is necessary to take into account the influence of several trends or currents of thought opposed to Christianity since the Renaissance, such as rationalist and atheistic humanism, spiritualist and esoteric movements, strident "secularization," positivistic "scientism," and so on. But the fact remains that Europe and North America were profoundly shaped by the Christian religion.

Under the pretext of their God-given dominion over nature, the "Christians" of this supposed Christian civilization often contributed to its overexploitation; they have at times crossed all too readily the threshold of overconsumption. Since such is so, they are in some respects responsible for the ecological crisis. They have abused nature and have allowed the situation to worsen without intervening; they have not exercised their creation-care mandate in conformity with the new "commandments" of love and justice revealed in Jesus Christ.

This sad state of affairs is underscored by Jacques Ellul, who is sometimes considered one of the heralds of modern ecology:

Man belongs to creation, but he should bring to it a sense of God's presence, which is why he is often called the *overseer* of creation on God's behalf. He is thus the Lieu-tenant[10] of God

---

[10] Ellul is referencing here the etymology of the word *lieutenant*, which literally means in French "place holder," for a lieutenant is an of-

over creation. . . . He must not oversee this creation for himself, in his own interests, according to his own personal viewpoints. . . . It seems to me that two boundary points must be recognized here: First of all, there is the fact that the authority of man is precisely limited by that of God. He is therefore in no wise truly master. The second aspect is that if man is to represent God, it stands to reason that he should exercise dominion over creation exactly *in the manner* that God does. It is not merely a delegation of *power* he receives . . . it is also a delegation *means:* in other words, if God guides his creation with love, by love, and for the purpose of Love, the same should apply to man. . . . He must not oversee creation for power and domination alone, but as a representative of the love of God.[11]

Church history has not been without some positive models: religious communities—such as the monks of many monasteries or the Mennonites or the Amish in Germany (and in Alsace) and then in America—have maintained, generally speaking, a different relationship with nature. These faithful men and women have shown themselves more respectful of human and natural limits, more critical vis-à-vis technological progress, often for both religious and social reasons (preservation of the Amish communal identity, for example), although there are delicate differences among these same communities. But are these models applicable to the church at large, especially in periods of strong economic growth?

Non-Christians and the Ecological Crisis

The results are mixed for different societies and traditions under the influence of other religions or governed by different philosophical and ideological principles.

---

ficer who takes command in lieu of a captain.—Trans.

[11] Jacques Ellul, "Le rapport de l'homme à la Création selon la Bible," *Foi et Vie* 75, no. 5–6 (1974): 138–39.

The East, which is reputed to be more mindful of nature and rightly so in many cases, has ended up falling into the same trap as Western countries, notably in Buddhist and Shintoistic Japan, to judge by the many environmental problems that exist in large urban areas and on the coasts.

Many extol the virtues of the Native Americans who lived in relative equilibrium with nature before the arrival of the European colonists. But was not this "animist" harmony—often idealized—due to their superstitious fear of the "spirits" of nature? Would this way of life have endured a more intense population growth, necessitating the nourishment, clothing, and housing of a greater number of individuals in optimal conditions? Otherwise, it must be claimed that the natural selection linked to epidemics and frequent conflicts between native clans was an efficacious means for favoring this symbiosis with nature.

Certain political ideologies, such as atheistic communism in the former Soviet Union and the old communist bloc of East Europe or in the China of not-too-long ago, pushed industry leaders to manipulate nature without restraint. They sought to twist nature to conform it to the output requirements of unrealistic economic models. The ecological situation of these regions is now often disastrous, even presenting in certain cases serious dangers for current and future populations. This is apparent in the unprecedented economic growth in China, which has amplified urban pollution, especially due to unbridled industrialization, electricity production in coal-fired power plants (which have proliferated in recent years), and automobile traffic. At a time when some are rediscovering, in major cities and in rural areas of Western nations, the benefits of walking and biking, the Chinese have abandoned their former virtuous habits in order to move about now in an asphyxiating haze of fumes laden with harmful particles from coal combustion and urban traffic jams. It seems, however, that the recently rising awareness with respect to the consequences these various pollutants, especially concerning health, is beginning to bear fruit and to incentivize the Chinese authorities to reduce, if possible, their principal contributors.

Countries in the Southern Hemisphere—whether they be under animist, Muslim, Hindu, or Christian influence—are starting to see their environment deteriorate for still other reasons, which have to do with poverty, the lack of financial means, and corruption, not to mention the absence of appropriate (and applicable) legislation to fight against pollution or the degradation of natural habitats. The negative consequences of over-cultivation, burn farming, and land clearing in Africa are being felt more and more in the now-degraded soils.

Finally, the negative impact of colonization must be cited when speaking of the ecological chaos of the Global South (i.e., loss of forest and wildlife, commercial monocropping, etc.), as well as the impact of ethnic rivalries and unsound domestic policies. Furthermore, these countries are often targeted by Western nations to recycle their most unwanted waste in questionable if not unacceptable circumstances. It is also in these countries that the most polluting production facilities are outsourced, leaving the impression that the most harmful and toxic substances are reserved for poor populations to handle so that the richest might live in optimal work and health conditions.

Radical Ecology

The most radical proponents of "deep ecology" consider the environmental safety measures that are commonly proposed to be superficial, both on a philosophical and practical level. They assert that humanity is corrupted and that it is necessary, in order to truly preserve biodiversity, to act "in-depth" and to change paradigms or worldviews. From their perspective, then, humans must renounce their anthropocentrism, be it Christian or no, in order to replace it with a "biocentrism" (or geocentrism) more in keeping with an advanced postmodern civilization. The human species thus finds itself relegated to the periphery of the system. It is no more than a speck of dust on an earth that precedes it in time and that will survive it. Thus population decrease, if not the disappearance of the human species, would then foster biodiversity since humans are the principal cause of the current disturbances in nature. They call for the recognition of a specific right (legally binding!) of animals, even plants and other organisms, to confront the threats posed by the humans who exploit them.

Certainly, it is jarring, and in some instances unconscionable, to see animals treated today like consumer goods that must be fattened and slaughtered in record time, under questionable circumstances, in order to be delivered as rapidly as possible and at the best price to consumers. (But what regard is there for quality?) Is it legitimate to raise genetically modified livestock (cattle, pigs, and poultry in particular) in order to enhance a return on investment, rounded up as they are by the hundreds in "factories" and confined in cramped "above-ground" enclosures where they never see natural light, stuffed with "artificial" feeds often supplemented with preventative treatments (mainly antibiotics), and slaughtered in the end on an assembly line like crude machine parts? Condemning animal suffering, so sadly true, is not to indulge in naive sentimentality. It can lead to legislation in favor of farm animals, which it sometimes does—but from there to then bestow on animals the "right" to turn on their "executioners"? It remains questionable, if not impossible, to attribute to mute animals (that are incapable of all rational communication) the privilege of "defending" themselves. The responsibility falls on human beings to make proper use of their freedom to rule over the animal kingdom. The biocentrism of deep ecology can carry them well beyond what is reasonable.

This extreme ecological philosophy could, in effect, lead to a frightening form of dictatorship. In his book *The New Ecological Order* (*Le nouvel ordre écologique*), Luc Ferry sees the danger of *deep* ecology and cites as an example Jean Fréchaut, who was for a time a member of the Green Party and who openly fantasized about "oppressing communities so as to reduce all pollution and change their desires and behaviors through psychological manipulation."[12]

---

[12] Luc Ferry, *Le nouvel ordre écologique: l'arbre, l'animal et l'homme* (Paris: Grasset, 1992), 127.

The "Extinction Rebellion" movement, born in Great Britain in 2018 and now international, claims its radicalism to "fight against ecological collapse and global warming." Its activists want to tackle the roots of the ecological and social problem. They want to make as many people as possible aware of the seriousness of the ecological crisis, which is resulting in the rapid extinction of species. They demand that the destruction of ecosystems cease and that carbon emissions be reduced and stopped as soon as possible. Their mode of action, which is allegedly nonviolent, is based on civil disobedience and aims to occupy public or private places, often linked to an activity that is harmful to the environment. Their goal is to "create a world that is fit for the next 7 generations to live in," and so to establish "a beautiful and healthy world, where individuality and creativity are encouraged, where we work and solve problems together, where everyone finds meaning, with courage, strength and love." This will be based on cultures rooted in respect for nature, true freedom, and social justice. The expected change, a true "regeneration," can begin when the minimum threshold of 3.5% of the population ready to mobilize (within their ranks) is reached. The rejection of hierarchy and centralization must encourage the autonomy of each individual and the participation of all in the decisions and actions to be taken (according to French and American "ExtinctionRebellion" websites). How far, however, can this new utopia take us? In many ways, we can partly sympathize with the sincere desire expressed by these activists to preserve the environment by living in a way that is better adapted to the resources of our planet, but is this all-human "rebellion" the best way to achieve this?

Biblical "Theocentrism"

In light of this, the biblical worldview appears more balanced and positive—in other words, more conducive to living. It is not centered on humanity, the earth, or nature: it is *theocentric*, centered on God, for he alone is true Lord, the absolute master of the earth. At the time of Moses, this ownership of the "earth" was meant to be taken literally, since every inch of land belonged in the first instance to God himself (Lev. 25:23). Without calling into question the notion of private property (or rather property that was "family owned"), which the Israelites were obliged to respect ("You shall not covet what belongs to your neighbor"; Exod. 20:17), they were also summoned to evaluate land pricing on the basis of the number of years between purchase date and the Feast of Jubilee, which took place every fifty years (Lev. 25:8–55). This festival could lead to a bona fide "land reform," a redistribution at least in part of properties so as to lift up the downtrodden, whether they were so due to adverse weather conditions or poor self-management. In any case, it was an opportunity to "swipe the slate clean" and to prevent runaway inflation in land pricing, not to mention questionable land speculation. But one cannot compare the biblical theocracy (under the old covenant regime) with our modern democracies and derive economic models from them in the strict sense.

It is therefore with God as ultimate reference point, and not humanity or nature, that Christians must live and regulate their behavior. Theocentrism should keep them from an overreaching power grab or other "centrisms" focused exclusively on man or nature. Must humanity die that nature might live? That opinion is not yet shared, thankfully, by the public generally speaking, and the Christian viewpoint remains promising to them for a workable mode of living in this present world, even if the Christian faithful have not always been its best witnesses—far from it, sadly.

The gospel is not thereby diminished in the process, however, for it does not depend on humanity but on God alone, who is the author and the guarantor of its effectiveness, for the salvation of the world. The gospel provides a gateway for the full reconciliation of human beings, as much with God as with their fellow humans and nature. Biblical and Christian faith can thus inspire the most beneficial protective measures for the environment; it is a fountain of hope for the whole creation. But Christians have not always viewed, at least not in the same manner, the gospel's effects to be the best for this world just as it is for the world to come.

5

ECOLOGY AND
"NEW CREATION"

For the creation waits in eager expectation for the children of God to be revealed. For the creation was subjected to frustration, not by its own choice, but by the will of the one who subjected it, in hope that the creation itself will be liberated from its bondage to decay and brought into the freedom and glory of the children of God. We know that the whole creation has been groaning as in the pains of childbirth right up to the present time. Not only so, but we ourselves, who have the firstfruits of the Spirit, groan inwardly as we wait eagerly for our adoption to sonship, the redemption of our bodies. (Rom. 8:19–23)

But the day of the Lord will come like a thief. The heavens will disappear with a roar; the elements will be destroyed by fire, and the earth and everything done in it will be laid bare. Since everything will be destroyed in this way, what kind of people ought you to be? You ought to live holy and godly lives as you look forward to the day of God and speed its coming. That day will bring about the destruction of the heavens by fire, and the elements will melt in the heat. But in keeping with his promise we are looking forward to a new heaven and a new earth, where righteousness dwells. (2 Pet. 3:10–13)

At first glance, these two passages seem to contradict one another: Paul lays emphasis on the *continuity* between the old and the new creation, while Peter emphasizes the *discontinuity*. In other words, will the earth and the sky completely disappear so as to be supplanted by a "new earth and new heavens"? Or, on the contrary, will this present creation subsist, at least in part, after what is called the "Day of the Lord"? How we view these two options with have definite consequences for ecology.

The Resurrection: From the Old Body to the New

If we consider biblical teaching in its totality, especially in light of the plan of salvation that God has wrought throughout the course of human history, it makes more sense to seek out the consistencies in the sacred texts rather than in their supposed contradictions. Now, the central event, the absolute reference point in the teaching of Paul as well as in that of Peter, and indeed in the entire Bible, remains the gospel. Jesus is God made man. He came into this world with a *body in the likeness* of that of every human being. He died by suffering the *physical and mental* torture of a criminal on a Roman cross. He was raised *bodily* the third day.

Jesus returned from the grave in a body at once "like and unlike" the human body. His disciples were able to recognize him and even touch him, but this same body had supernatural properties since it allowed him to join his disciples in their usual meeting place without passing through doors. Nevertheless, Jesus nourished his body after the resurrection: he ate with his disciples (Luke 24:36–43; John 21:9–13) and then he ascended into heaven, still in bodily and visual form. He was therefore in no wise a disembodied "spirit."

According to the Christian creed, which is drawn from the New Testament on precisely these points, Jesus "sat on the right hand of God" (Mark 16:19) from whence he reigns, which means that he shares with the Father the role of Lord over creation. In the end, he shall return "in the same way" that he departed (Acts 1:11), which is to say in bodily form. He shall also appear "in blazing fire" (2 Thess. 1:7) to "judge the living and the dead" (2 Tim. 4:1), and to establish the eternal reign of his Father, when at last all his enemies shall bow the knee before him (1 Cor. 15:24).

The event of the resurrection of Jesus is fundamental for a clear understanding of the discontinuity as well as the continuity that exist between the old and the new creation.[1] In 1 Corinthians 15:20, the apostle Paul writes that Jesus, the Christ (the Messiah), is as it were the "firstfruits"—based on the Old Testament notion of offering the first agricultural produce of the harvest—of those who have died and who are going to return to life again. The resurrection of men and women will follow then a process similar to that of Jesus, who rose triumphantly when he passed from death to life.

The old body will indeed die, but its return to life will occur in a new body, or more precisely in the present body, but which will then be regenerated, transformed, made incorruptible, unable to be affected by evil, immortal. Paul specifies to the Corinthians that this is because it is a "spiritual body," a body vivified by the Spirit of God, reflecting the very glory of God, and thus rendering to human beings their first vocation to be fully "in the image of God."

This transition from the old to the new body will be brought about through "the power of God" (1 Cor. 6:14). As Paul states in his Epistle to the Philippians: "[God] will transform our lowly body to be like his glorious body, by the power that enables him even to subject all things to himself" (3:21 ESV). In the Epistle to the Romans, he adds: "If the Spirit of him who raised Jesus from the dead dwells in you, he who raised Christ Jesus from the dead will also give life to your mortal bodies through his Spirit who dwells in you" (8:11 ESV).

There is then both discontinuity and continuity between the old body tainted by sin, subject to evil, mortal, and the new body that will be liberated from the consequences of sin and hence immortal. The body will pass from one state to another, just as a grain of wheat passes into a plant state, as Paul suggests in using this metaphor (1 Cor. 15:35–54). The doctrine of "the resurrection of the body," as stated in the Apostles' Creed, is of primary importance here; for it is not only the "soul" that is saved but the entire being—body and soul.

---

[1] See Sylvain Romerowski, "L'avenir de la terre," in *La fin d'un monde. Quel avenir pour l'homme et son environnement* (Marne-la-Vallée/Paris: Farel/GBU, 2012), 53–63.

The process will be somewhat similar on a creation-wide scale, for as Paul writes in Romans: "For the creation waits in eager expectation for the children of God to be revealed. . . . The creation itself will be liberated from its bondage to decay and brought into the freedom and glory of the children of God" (8:19, 21). Paul employs the same terms here as he does in 1 Corinthians 15 concerning the bodily resurrection of the individual believer; it will therefore be a kind of "resurrected creation."

Consequently, there is a link between the resurrection of Jesus and believers in him and the resurrection of creation of which Jesus is also the "firstborn," the "firstfruits," and the "new Adam." The situation of human beings today is analogous to that of the earth in the present age and what it will be in the age to come. The entire creation suffers the consequences of sin (the ground is "cursed" following the fall; see Gen. 3:17–18) and it awaits its deliverance.

Continuity

In order to illustrate the painful passage from the old to the new creation, Paul compares it to the pangs of a pregnant woman about to give birth (Rom. 8:22–24). He then adds that "we ourselves groan within ourselves, waiting for the adoption" (KJV). This last term refers to the fact that those who have placed their faith in God and in Jesus the Messiah-Savior will at last be fully recognized as "children of God," *adopted* by the Father. This is precisely the "revelation of the children of God" that the earth awaits with impatience and in suffering. Now, Paul had just declared, right before this passage (vv. 15–16), that by faith in Jesus, men and women are *already* children of God, so that they can call God "*Abba*," which signifies in Aramaic "Father." And yet he seems to then turn around and state that these very "children" must still wait for God to make them his children!

To express both this simultaneity and distance in time, some theologians have coined the phrase "already and not yet," which refers to the present time between the resurrection of Jesus and that of his return to earth. Christians are already children of God, and more or less visibly so, by virtue of their faith in Jesus, but they are not yet children of God in the full sense of the term; for they await the day when all creation will become fully conscious of this fact, when Christians can "see with their own eyes" that they are truly children of their Lord.

It will be then, as Paul emphasizes, a veritable "unveiling" (the Greek term is translated by the English term "apocalypse"). This final revelation of God and of his children will bring about a deliverance of the entire creation, for Jesus will then complete his work of reconciliation between "all things" and the Creator (Col. 1:20), as a kind of "summation." The world will again be placed under the Lord's reign. The glorious Messiah, now definitively conqueror, will erase all evil and its consequences forever. Jesus himself, the prophets, and the apostles had announced this deliverance in advance (Hos. 13:14; Isa. 25:8; Luke 20:36; 1 Cor. 15:26, 55). Regenerated human beings, both body and soul, will finally be able to manage this creation without the tainting effects of sin. They will therefore be able to truly take care of it for the glory of the Creator and for the benefit of the entire creation.

The entire earth will therefore take part in the redemption won by Jesus Christ. The "Lamb of God" did not only die to expiate the sins of individual humans so that their offenses might be forgiven and so that they might have access to God and be able to know him and indeed love him as their Father, but he has also risen from the grave so that creation might be liberated from evil and restored:

The New Testament employs several terms to describe the otherness of the world to come: "regeneration" (*palingenesia*, Matt 19:28), "freedom" (*eleutherōthēsetai*, Rom 8:21), "vanishing form" (*paragei to schēma*, 1 Cor 7:31), "restoration" (*apokatastasis*, Act 3:21). It provides a glimpse into the difference between the current order and that perfection in every sense of what has been promised, all within a framework of continuity-discontinuity and ultimate fulfillment.[2]

_____

[2] Samuel Bénétreau, *La Deuxième Épître de Pierre, l'Épître de Jude*, CEB (Vaux-sur-Seine: Édifac, 1994), 208. See also by the same author,

In the present age, creation suffers and longs for its deliverance. We have only a foretaste of reconciliation with God, a first glimpse of this deliverance. By faith in Jesus, and all the more so if this faith is put into practice, it is already possible to see the beneficial effects of a still-partial restoration (or of a "putting back together") of the relationships between human beings and God, their neighbors, and their environment (Isa. 11:7–9; 67:17–25; Apoc. 21:1–4). But creation, in the human and natural environment, continues to endure the consequences of evil and thus to suffer hardship. Between the old and the new creation, Jesus' first "mission" is to return to earth to "judge the living and the dead."

It is precisely this theme of judgment, exemplified by the image of fire, that Peter highlights in order to describe the discontinuity between creation in its present state and the new creation to come.

Discontinuity

Before considering the differences between the texts of Peter and of Paul, it is best to begin by pointing out their similarities. Peter is conscious of expressing a point of view similar to Paul concerning the patience of God, the return of Jesus Christ, the final judgment, and the expectation of the last day that will come "like a thief." This last day will also be a new beginning. Peter concludes his teaching in these terms: "Bear in mind that our Lord's patience means salvation, just as our dear brother Paul also wrote you with the wisdom that God gave him" (2 Pet. 3:15).

Indeed, Paul often discusses the theme of judgment, in similar terms at times to those used here by Peter, in particular when he states that Jesus will return to earth "in blazing fire" (2 Thess. 1:7). Paul compares himself to a wise architect who built the house of God upon a solid foundation, on the gospel of Jesus Christ (1 Cor. 3:10–11). Now, in this same chapter, Paul reminds his readers that

"Critique de la thèse d'un anthropocentrisme biblique écologiquement ravageur," 51–80.

all the works of men and women who build the house of God will be "tested by fire" (v. 13), to see if they can stand the test and if they are worthy of the "kingdom of God"—of the world to come, at last under the visible reign of God.

According to context, since these works are undertaken in the wake of the gospel, they are like an extension of the "house of God," founded on the cornerstone laid by Jesus himself and also on which all things rests (1 Cor. 3:10–15; 2 Thess. 1:5–10; 1 Pet. 1:7; Rev. 21:24–26; Isa. 60). Fire then permits us to see what will withstand this decisive test. If the house is built with straw, it will be consumed. But if it is built with solid stone, it will hold fast. Fire is the image of the judgment of God over the works and the attitudes of those who participate in the construction of the house of God by proclaiming the gospel and by discipling Christians, the "living stones" of the temple of God (1 Pet. 2:5).

Jesus himself, Paul, Peter, and John, as well as several prophets of the Old Testament such Isaiah, all mention this major discontinuous event introduced by divine judgment: "Heaven and earth will pass away" (Matt. 24:35) or "disappear" (Rev. 21:1 TLB). Peter states that they will be *destroyed (luó*, the Greek verb, is used three times). According to certain Greek language specialists, it would be more accurate to translate this verb as "dissolved" (ESV). Peter further specifies that heaven and earth will be "liquefied" or even "melted" (*tēketai*) (2 Pet. 3:7–12). But his intention is not to frighten his readers; rather, it is to reassure them.

An Encouragement for Christians

It is thus important to delve into the deeper meaning of these verses, and its verbs in particular, by taking into account the full context of the chapter and indeed of the entire Epistle.

The primary intention of Peter here is to exhort his fellow believers not to pay heed to what non-Christians were claiming about the Lord's promise—namely, that he would return to earth and bring about a complete "healing" or "deliverance" to humankind and creation. They mocked this, saying, "Where is this 'coming' he promised? Ever since our ancestors died, everything goes on as it has since the beginning of creation" (2 Pet. 3:4).

The same critique is still being leveled today! Just as at the time of Moses or in the parable of Jesus, the master seems to "delay in coming." Some use this as a pretext to tolerate evil, engage in debauchery and in the idolatry of the "golden calf," as if they no longer had hope (Exod. 32; Matt. 24:48–49).

To respond to this sneering critique, Peter evokes the specter of the first flood, as Jesus also taught:

> "Just as it was in the days of Noah, so also will it be in the days of the Son of Man. People were eating, drinking, marrying and being given in marriage up to the day Noah entered the ark. Then the flood came and destroyed them all. It was the same in the days of Lot. People were eating and drinking, buying and selling, planting and building. But the day Lot left Sodom, fire and sulfur rained down from heaven and destroyed them all. It will be just like this on the day the Son of Man is revealed."
>
> (Luke 17:26–30)

It should be noted here that the watery flood and the rain of fire are both taken by Jesus as *examples*, since these two early cataclysms did not destroy all things, but only a portion of this world or a certain segment of humanity.

A Teaching on Vigilance

In Jesus' teaching, however, just as in Peter's Epistle, emphasis is laid most especially on the *unpredictable suddenness* of his return. The day shall come "like a thief." Peter thus recalls the Lord's warning: "But understand this: If the owner of the house had known at what hour the thief was coming, he would not have let his house be broken into. You also must be ready, because the Son of Man will come at an hour when you do not expect him" (Luke 12:39–40).

Moreover, at the time, Peter had taken the matter particularly to heart in posing this question: "Lord, are you telling this parable to us, or to everyone?" (12:41). He did not forget the response of his master—namely, the parable of the servant who says to himself, "My master is taking a long time in coming," and who then begins to beat the other servants, whom he oversees, and to eat and drink and become inebriated. The master of that servant, as Jesus admonishes again, will come "on a day when he does not expect him and at an hour he is not aware of" (12:45–46).

In his long discourse, taking the form of a solemn warning and linked to his return and judgment, Jesus declares to have come "to bring fire on the earth" (Luke 12:49), as if the first flames of that fire were already being felt. As Jesus says elsewhere, "For judgment I have come into this world, so that the blind will see and those who see will become blind" (John 9:39). It must not be forgotten, though, apart from this "fiery" discourse, the other exhortation of the Lord and later that of his disciples. For it is mainly to encourage his contemporaries to receive the salvation that he brings that Jesus addresses them: "If anyone hears my words but does not keep them, I do not judge that person. For I did not come to judge the world, but to save the world" (John 12:47).

Peter insists then on the necessity for Christians to remain vigilant so that they might not be caught unawares by this day, which they await without knowing precisely the hour (which God alone knows; Mark 13:32) and which will come "like a thief."

The Earth Exposed to Judgment

Finally, it is verse 10 in 2 Peter 3 that poses the most difficulty, for there are several variants in the most ancient manuscripts for the verb often translated as indicating consumption by fire: "the earth also and the works that are therein shall be *burned up*" (KJV; cf. RSV, NASB, etc.).

Now, in some ancient manuscripts, this verb is simply not mentioned. Others have a different verb that can be otherwise translated: "the earth will be ... *laid bare*" (NIV). If such is so, then it should be understood that the earth will be "exposed" (ESV)—exposed to scrutiny, without being able to hide. It cannot be excluded that there is an allusion here to the judgment of God: the earth will be laid bare to the scrutiny *of God*, or more exactly his *judgment*. Might there also be an allusion to this very judgment in the image of the "eyes ... like as blazing fire," described by John when he sees the "Son of man" in the book of Revelation (1:14)? Can we also relate this "nakedness" to the awareness of nakedness and the shame Adam and Eve felt when they were exposed to God's judgment after eating the fruit of the "tree of the knowledge of good and evil"?

Whatever the case, several translators adopt this last clause: "But the day of the Lord will come like a thief, and then the heavens will pass away with a loud noise, and the elements will be dissolved with fire, and the earth and everything that is done on it will be *disclosed*" (NRSV) or "will be found to deserve *judgment*" (NLT).

Peter does not specifically declare that heaven and earth will be obliterated, but rather that they will pass from one state to another when they are exposed to the judgment of God, symbolized by fire. Heaven and earth do not disappear then per se, since this creation "groans as in the pains of childbirth," as Paul writes; but they shall be radically transformed, just as newborns come into the world. They may waste away due to corruption, to sin that results in the judgment of God and death. But they will reappear—they will be restored—in a new condition; they will become incorruptible, they will be regenerated by the power of the Lord, and they will return to life in the wake of the resurrection of Jesus.

Again, the purifying element may be fire, which is very often in the Bible the imagery associated with the judgment of God or of his holiness, for God cannot be corrupted by evil. This fire literally causes the elements to melt (*tēketai*), but it does not thereby reduce them to ashes. Earth and sky are purified just as metals are passed through fire, and it is therefore sin, that *agent* of corruption, the works of sin (the earth and its works), as well as sinners themselves (v. 7) that are subject to this fire and *exposed* to divine judgment.

A New Creation "in Jesus Christ"

From this judgment, a new pure creation will emerge, rid of all uncleanness of its dross, and a new "temple" will arise, a new "city" that the holy God can fully inhabit and rule over as uncontested Lord (Eph. 2:11–22; Rev. 21 and 22; etc.). God does not destroy his creation that he has deemed good (*tôv*) from the beginning, but he *delivers* it from evil, just as he does for all believers. He liberates it from the "slavery" of sin, by virtue of the death and resurrection of the Messiah/Christ and by the power of the Holy Spirit (Rom. 6). As in the beginning, he desires to "cover" human beings and the whole creation with his grace as with a new and strong garment (Gen. 3:21).

The prospect of "end" is therefore not an excuse to consider that, since "everything will vanish," it is not necessary to care for human beings and nature in this world. On the contrary, Christians should make every effort to safeguard creation, for they already benefit from that redemption that will extend to the entire universe. The same holds true for this present life, for the physical body that, although it is mortal, everyone takes care of each and every day. And this also concerns spiritual life: Peter exhorts the recipients of his letter to nurture their relationship with God in the expectation of the grand denouement: "Since everything will be destroyed in this way, what kind of people ought you to be? You ought to live holy and godly lives" (2 Pet. 3:11). The protection of the environment is a part of this holy and godly mode of living, and it should be the outcome of a serene and refreshing relationship with the Creator.

From the moment of their conversion, Christians are children of God the Father, through faith in Jesus the Son (Rom. 8:16–17). They are literally a "new creation in Jesus Christ" (2 Cor. 5:17)—Jesus himself being the "firstborn" of this new creation, the cornerstone or the foundation of the building. They can therefore bear the firstfruits of the presence of God in their lives by his Spirit.

The apostle Paul provides a list (not exhaustive) of these "fruits of the Spirit" in Galatians 5:22: love, joy, peace, forbearance, kindness, goodness, faithfulness, gentleness, and self-control. These "spiritual" qualities certainly have positive effects on the relationship between human beings and nature. They constitute the firstfruits of the revelation of the children of God, albeit still partial, and the beginning of the healing that can be brought even now to his creation that suffers from evil and its consequences in the world.

The ideal of the law is to love both God and neighbor (Deut. 6:5; Lev. 19:18). The gospel, the good news of the salvation in Jesus Christ, is reflected and applied by doing good to fellow human beings and by the wise management of natural resources. The gospel leads Christians thereby to witness to their faith as a sign of their hope: Jesus, the Messiah, will one day bring about a full healing to the entire creation. The continuity between the old and the new creation gives meaning to what they accomplish in this world *for* this world.

The question of the "end times" remains, however, a delicate issue—in particular on a theological and philosophical level, as it will have practical consequences with respect to the environment in the world today.

6

ESCHATOLOGY
AND ECOLOGY

Christians today have rather different conceptions of what theologians have dubbed (especially since the mid-nineteenth century) "eschatology" or the study of the "end times." Eschatology concerns the mortal decay, divine judgment, and physical resurrection of all human beings, and thus the passage from one reality to the next.

It is also centered on the "Second Coming" (or the "appearance," from the Greek word *Parousia*) of Jesus Christ and the definitive establishment of his "reign" or "kingdom." The conceptual differences among Christians hinge on two key points: the *time* and the *place* where this "end" will occur. As we have seen, the "end" can be considered as a continuation or a new beginning.

Non-Christians have devised their own various visions of the future. The influence of certain religious and philosophical trends has made itself felt on Christian thought and vice versa, so the diverse points of view overlap at times.

Several of these have rallied together to assert that man is building himself a brighter future on earth: he will establish a new "golden age," with or without the "outside" help of God or a "divine power." Others, on the contrary, beg to differ and make a radical distinction between "heaven" and "earth" and their own future. Each perspective has its consequences with respect to the way we live in this world and the way we harness and protect the environment.

Philosophical Materialism

Atheistic and materialistic evolutionism accords a prominent place to blind chance and deterministic forces through the sifting process of natural selection, as well as to the progress resulting from the agency of human beings governed by autonomous reason. "Evil" is therefore reduced to the impersonal role of history working itself out, which permits civilization, as if by reaction to world events, to advance toward a greater "good." But here these two notions of good and evil remain highly relative.

The result of this line of thinking is a strictly mechanistic vision of the world. The task of men and women is thus to fully understand the cause-and-effect relationships of nature, to make them their own, so as to ameliorate the conditions of life here on earth. This understanding remains, to be sure, the basis of all scientific enquiry, a starting point that is not necessarily a bad thing in itself.

Atheistic materialists generally agree that religion is an invention based on moral ideals that grant, at best, access to a sort of higher plane of human and social evolution. This process rests on the notion that the "man-god," actual or in the process of becoming, is alone master of this earth, which he gradually transforms, if possible, into a comfortable "paradise" for all humanity.

This materialistic trend, grafting at times onto various political movements, might tend eventually to favor significant environmental protection initiatives; but also, the very opposite can be true: totalitarian ideologies, alas, offered shameful examples of the latter in Eastern Europe and in Asia throughout the twentieth century.

The philosophy that drives atheistic materialism can scarcely curb the voraciousness of the human appetite, which has led to the overexploitation of nature for more than a century. When this overexploitation is seconded by unbridled hedonism on a personal level, it can lead to the most harmful excesses. Each individual seeks to "profit" from nature in an entirely self-serving manner. Its benefits are usually reserved, though, for the effete few who have somehow managed to turn the randomness of evolution to their advantage. And whenever a more egalitarian distribution of resources is proposed, it tends to be imposed by force, which means that the former totalizing worldview (i.e., religious) is replaced by another aggressive form of utopianism (i.e., ideological, political, economic, ecological, etc.).

This materialistic bent can also be faulted for a lack of long-term perspective, deleterious for the environment from the time it is appropriated within one or two generations. It should finally be observed that materialism has difficulty providing, unless by imposition, an ethical framework for the populations over which such a philosophy holds sway. Each individual can therefore believe that the mastery of the natural environment is without limit, and thus that all the biological borders can be overstepped for research purposes, especially those in the medical domain, provided it "serves humanity," as the most idealistic and best-intentioned proponents hope.

This trend is rivaled nowadays by a "spiritualist" movement, in part because materialism has been criticized as a new form of "religiosity," with all its quasi-religious forms of expression (such as the cult of personality), which ironically only goes to prove that human beings cannot escape the spiritual dimension wherever they turn.

Spiritualist Philosophy

Spiritualist evolutionism integrates a divine dimension in this process. "God" is thus "defined" as a universal consciousness-intelligence, scattered, and impersonal permeating the universe in all its aspects. This "divine" cosmic ensemble moves forward toward the ultimate goal of an ever-expanding evolution and complexity of processes and organisms, as a result of an "upward" or "cohesive" movement. This is a form of pantheism, in which God is confused with the universe.

The dualism of certain philosophies may converge, in another form, with this worldview. A distinction is then made between spirit (or God), considered as what is "good," and matter, which represents "evil" or what is "bad." They are juxtaposed, opposed, and in perpetual conflict. During the first centuries of the Christian era, Neoplatonic philosophies and gnostic trends thus described, while extending it, the process of "emanation of God in matter" of the "descent of the One unfolding itself in the many and the rising of the many which return to the One."

This is also the case, based on different viewpoints and from diverse perspectives, with respect to trends as well as mystic and esoteric writings such as the Jewish (or Christian) kabbalah and the Hindu Vedas, or even religious philosophies such as Taoism and Buddhism.

The Pantheism of Spinoza

A more recent pantheistic current of thought has attached itself to the philosophy of Spinoza (1632–77), which considered that God and nature are one. This "naturalistic" worldview is in fact rationalistic: it is produced by human reason, though it is elaborated within a spiritualist framework. This doctrine could be described as a sort of "pantheistic agnosticism." God cannot be known since he is not personal, nor is he indistinguishable from nature. Again, this represents an abbreviated version of a more complex philosophy, but it influences a great many of our contemporaries who wish to introduce a "spiritual" note to their materialistic worldview, in which "heaven" is *melded* with "earth." Their "world-god" has high-profile proponents these days among scientists, artists, and writers. Einstein himself claimed to be influenced by Spinozan philosophy, which he preferred to faith in a personal God.

Process Theology

In a similar vein, Process Theology, fashionable in our postmodern times, has undeniable affinities with the current evolutionist, dialectic, and integrated worldview. This theology regards "God" as not omniscient and as in the process of "becoming." He changes at the rhythm in which both the world and humanity change. He depends in part on human freedom and creativity, but also on the evolution of earth and nature. He identifies then with the history of the universe by being subject to the randomness and mutability of evolution. He extends himself, as it were, through all of these world experiences. He is at once outside and inside creation, but not in the same sense nor according to the same traditional theological categories of transcendence and immanence.

For some Process theologians, just as in Jewish mysticism, God is so reduced that he ends up eclipsing himself and becomes part and parcel of humanity here on earth. Thus Process Theology has an explanation for evil, and especially for the "absence" or the "silence" of God during the worst sufferings endured by humanity, especially when men are themselves the cause, such as during the Shoah, the Nazi genocide of the Jews.[1]

New Age

The nebulous New Age movements assimilate and synthetize the various philosophic and religious traditions (syncretism), including Asian religions, animism, and paganism. They consider the earth to be a divinity called "Gaia," thus elevating the earth to the rank of a mother goddess. Generally speaking, the adherents of these movements advocate a concern for nature that seems at first glance to be quite noble. But they draw inspiration, once again, from a pantheistic and Eastern view of nature—according to which one mustn't disturb a particular animal because it is deemed a particle of the divine, the reincarnation of an individual, man or woman, who has more or less conducted himself or herself well in a previous life.

---

[1] See Hans Jonas, "The Concept of God after Auschwitz," in *A Holocaust Reader: Responses to the Nazi Extermination*, ed. Michael L. Morgan (New York: Oxford University Press, 2001), 259–70.

These spiritualistic trends that recommend noninterference with nature are often driven by a mystical idealism, or in other cases, by fatalism or disenchanted cynicism, whose adverse effects can be observed in different populations and at times in nature, despised and neglected rather than cultivated with care. Good and evil are fused in a sort of opaque muddle, such that we can neither know the future nor the consequences on the world.

Panentheism

The spiritualist, or rather pantheist, conception of God can take a different form, which is more properly termed "panentheist": God is in everything in the world, within and without. To be sure, this "monist" view (all things are one) is far different from traditional biblical doctrine, according to which God is radically distinct from the world (i.e., he is transcendent or "beyond" the world) of which he is nevertheless the creator and the ruler, both immutable and eternal.

His presence in the world (i.e., his immanence: God dwells in the world that depends on him) is spiritual and *personal*. This distinction is well articulated in the phraseology of the church fathers in describing the Trinity as one God in three persons "distinct but not separate, united but not confused."

The Bible makes other distinctions as well: between the "earth" (our planet) and "heaven" (or "paradise," the "place" where God "dwells"); between the soul (spirit, heart) and the body; and between the present age (before the return of Christ) and the age to come (after the return of Christ). But these "dualities" are not marked by an opposition between good and evil or between what is right and what is wrong.

In practice, however, Christians accord undue weight to some of these dualistic views, notably in the realm of eschatology. This posture is not without ramifications for the manner in which they live in the world today and for the protection of the environment.

The Paradise of "Heaven"

A dualist and often naive conception of "heaven," as *opposed* (in a negative way) to this "world" or this "earth," remains pervasive in our Christian culture today. It appears in different forms, as well in other religions or philosophies.

Whether forward-looking or backward-looking to Golden Age myths, the radiant world glimpsed by Plato beyond the cave, or the divorce of matter and spirit, all of these conceptions continue to distort our Christian vision of the world and its future. From Neoplatonism and Gnosticism, which often influenced Christian thought in the early centuries of the church, the notion of a disembodied "heaven" or "kingdom of God" has persisted, disengaged from all matter associated with evil, as the place of incorporeal pure souls.

The contact points are again manifold with Eastern religions and philosophies that consider the material world as an *illusion*, putting greater emphasis on the spiritual realm, which is considered superior. This often results in a fatalistic attitude, a disinterest in the present life, a disparagement of the "things here below," or contempt for nature and the body. And as for the issue before us, this has led to a particular carelessness with respect to this earth, which should be cultivated, managed, and protected.

Christians are right to distinguish "heaven" from "earth," but matter and the human body are not "bad"; everything was created "good" by God. This remains true even after the fall, the severing of the covenant with God, when man and woman thought they could distinguish good from evil on an autonomous basis, irrespective of any relationship to or dependence on God.

Christians can thus have a positive view of this world, even in a dualist perspective, which should allow them to maintain a certain equilibrium in their relationship with the present and the future of the planet as well as its resources.

Intelligent Design

Some Christians, particularly in the United States, have sought to reconcile theories of evolution with their faith in a Creator God. They have thus endorsed, as have many non-Christians, the theory of "Intelligent Design."

Both express admiration for the astronomical arrangement of the universe and its cosmological constants essential for the equilibrium of the whole; or, on the contrary, they express awe for the complex subtleties of the minutest biological structures; or simply even, they marvel at the "beauties of nature." For these Christians and non-Christians, God (or some mastermind, some overarching intelligence) is the source of life, with a particular plan (or *design*), directing or controlling the evolution of the universe and leading it progressively to its ultimate end of perfection. For the adherents of this theory, the meaning of life and of this world as a whole is better explained by the intervention of an intelligent, causing agent than by the impersonal processes of chance, necessity, and natural selection.

The theory of Intelligent Design is most attractive when it integrates the latest scientific data concerning evolution. But this is not always the case. It is sometimes presented as a critique of Darwinism, at least in its "materialistic" form:

> The defenders of *Intelligent Design* maintain that Darwin inverted the sequence of events: "life" does not emerge by chance, in one way or the other, from a material or non-living substrate, but seems to have been continually present in matter in the form of information, which suggests that matter may be a derivative or second reality. Moreover, these apologists maintain that the information network contained in the simplest or the minutest living systems is so sophisticated and so "irreducibly complex" that it bears witness to the existence of a type of intelligence, all of which threatens the materialistic assumptions of Darwinian evolution.[2]

---

[2] Reed Davis, "Le dessein intelligent, une nouvelle critique de l'évolution darwinienne," *La Revue réformée*, no. 245 (2008): 1.

Some Christians have endeavored to ratify their theology with the stamp of this theory critical of Darwinism, since it buttressed their faith in a creator and providential God. But not all Christians are in agreement with respect to how God created the world.

Creationism

Intelligent Design has thus been criticized for providing scientific support, in particular in the United States, for "Creationism" to be established as a system of thought proper to being taught in schools and universities, on a par with theories of evolution. This has even become, in certain American states, a veritable political issue, which is rather surprising for a Frenchman or European citizen.

The word *Creationism*, however, is ambiguous. The true and the false are mixed together so as to render the traditional Christian position even more confused. In point of fact, Christians (in principal) all confess a same *credo*, they believe in one all-mighty God, "creator of heaven and earth." They are thus all "creationists"! But they are not all in agreement on the *manner* in which God created the world, in particular on the timeline of the process of creation.

By "creationists," to be sure, reference is most often made to those Christians who hold that God created the world in six twenty-four-hour days, according to a literal reading of the first chapters of Genesis, based on their trust in the omnipotence of God. Some prefer to see these "days" as six periods of varying length of time that "match," to a certain extent and broadly speaking, with the geological "ages" or the various stages of the appearance of life-forms on earth (although often these stages take place in a shorter time span, or so they think) to that determined in general by geologists and biologists.

A great many other Christians in the world prefer to rely on the most rigorous scientific data, revealing a longer dimension of time for life-forms to appear—14 billion years—which does not in any way contradict faith in an eternal Creator God. In view of the dimensions of the universe (ever in expansion), the number of galaxies that can be counted by the hundreds of billions, themselves containing hundreds of billions of suns and stars, all moving in a time-space with unfathomable dimensions (scientists even speak of possible "multiverses"!), these "astronomical" (!) figures lead those believers to worship a God for whom "a thousand years are like a day" (Ps. 90:4). They recognize that his thoughts and his acts "are higher than [their] thoughts" (Isa. 55:9); they far exceed human comprehension, even the most enlightened by science and by faith.

Creation and Evolution

Christian evolutionists are thus just as convinced that God "not only created all things, but that he governs and directs them, disposing and ordaining by his sovereign will all that happens in the world," according to the terms of the Calvinist La Rochelle Confession of Faith (1559). They consider the theory of evolution to be a reasonable hypothesis for explaining the origins and the development of diverse forms of life and matter on earth.

There are many, however, who are not satisfied with all the answers afforded by science. They especially question the simplistic answers sometimes offered by armchair scientists to account for morphological evolution and the diversification of species. Over-eager "adaptationists" sometimes make us wince when, for example, they seek at all costs to lay out the "scientific" reasons for the physical traits and behaviors of animals. Others do not shrink from putting a human face on the universe itself in order to offer an explanation for its "positive" evolution, oriented toward life. There is no easy escape from the notion of a creator and providential God! And Christians who profess their faith in this eternal God are not completely illogical, even when they sometimes defend controversial theses concerning the origin of the universe and the "timeline" of this creation.

In all events, faith in a creator God is a question of faith (Heb. 11:3)! This remains true even when we are simply amazed by the beauty, the undeniable harmony, and the very possibility of life in its diversified forms on earth. Finally, let us not forget that the first chapter of Genesis, in the context of the ancient Middle East, was especially a means of presenting a "good" God as unique, distinct from his creation and in relationship with his creatures. This God is radically different from the polymorphic and fickle gods of local mythology: he is the creator of the sun, the moon, the stars, the heavens, the earth, and the sea and the animals and plants that live in them, and most especially of human beings, man and woman, fashioned "in his image" to take care of this world.[3]

This extraordinary message, when it was delivered (first by oral tradition, probably as early as the second millennium before the Christian era), was a radical novelty likely to arouse the astonishment, even the amazement of the contemporaries of Abraham, Moses, or Ezra. This is indeed the absolute originality of the first chapter of Genesis.

A Good Reason for Protecting Nature

Intelligent Design does not offer any "scientific proof" of God, not beyond what can be gleaned from observation of nature or from the study of its origins, its evolution, and its most outstanding current characteristics. This theory should therefore be considered, at best, as part of the "common revelation" of God through creation, as we have seen in Romans 1:19–23.

It is thus possible to discern an "intentional pattern" in the structures of the universe and living beings. This is a viewpoint shared by Christians as well as by non-Christians, whether on a religious or philosophic basis or no (see, for example, the writings of the Buddhist astrophysicist Trinh Xuan Thuan). Every person can be receptive to the beauty and the complexity of nature, to the development

---

[3] On the question of a unique God as presented in the Bible compared with the gods of ancient Middle Eastern myths, see Matthieu Richelle, *Comprendre Genèse 1–11 aujourd'hui.*

of life in all its forms on earth, including the extraordinary vital power of the bacterial flagellum, so often wielded by the adherents of Intelligent Design as an irrefutable proof of their theory!

In any case, there is good reason for preserving and promoting biodiversity and, by extension, the protection of the environment. Herein lies without doubt the positive contribution that faith in a creator God can make, without dismissing those evolutionary theories that underscore the close relationship between creation and its evolution throughout time, and hence the need to preserve the species present today. These matters have to do with fundamental workings of life, and it is therefore legitimate to question the tinkering of man with respect to the genetic pool, including his very own.

The Beginning of the End

Still to be addressed is the "special revelation" of God in his son Jesus, the Messiah, true God and true man, whom Christians affirm to be the only mediator for knowing God, by grace. It is when these general and special "revelations" coincide that we gain added incentive to make every effort to care for what God has created. For the "Son of Man" has come to confirm the frequent appeals of the prophets, not to despise the weakest and most vulnerable creatures, as was first established by the social laws of Leviticus at the time of Moses. Now these laws, as we have already underscored, aimed to maintain equilibrium between the lifestyle of men and women and their environment.

As the "Son of God," Jesus came not only to cleanse the offenses of human beings and to correct all spiritual dysfunction brought about by the fall (the breaking of the covenant with God), but also to return to creation its original splendor. The "end times," in fact, began with the resurrection of Jesus on the morning of Easter. But the process is well underway, and it will continue to unfold until the return of the Savior and Lord to this world, which will thereby be radically transformed.

Just as with creation, Christians have different points of view concerning the end times. Let this not be then a pretext for incalcitrant divisiveness on anyone's part, for it is wholly unjustified. Now, there remains one last point to examine—namely, the various eschatological schemes elaborated by theologians over time based on the biblical data. We shall consider each of them briefly in turn while concentrating on their practical consequences for the protection of the environment.[4]

Three Eschatological Frameworks

From the first centuries, the disciples of Jesus Christ have attempted to penetrate the mysteries surrounding the "end times," referenced by Jesus and the various authors of the New Testament. Their speculations have revolved in particular around the notion of the "millennium"—the period of a thousand years, real or symbolic, mentioned by John in in the book of Revelation (20:2–7).

Each of the following principal eschatological frameworks constructed by theologians have consequences for the safeguarding of creation in the present era.

Postmillennialism

"Postmillennialists" consider that the "time of the church," between the first and the second advent of Christ, coincides with the symbolic period of a thousand years referenced by John. During this age, Jews and non-Jews who constitute the church (literally, according to the Greek *ecclēsia*: the *assembly* of those who have believed in Jesus, who have recognized him as the Messiah) become more and more numerous. They are the fruit of the practical application of the "missionary mandate" left by Jesus to his disciples:

---

[4] For a more detailed study, see Henri Blocher, *L'espérance chrétienne*, Éclairages (Vaux-sur-Seine/Charols: Édifac/Excelsis, 2012).

"All authority in heaven and on earth has been given to me. Therefore, go and make disciples of all nations, baptizing them in the name of the Father and of the Son and of the Holy Spirit, and teaching them to obey everything I have commanded you. And surely, I am with you always, to the very end of the age."

(Matt. 28:18–20)

The influence of Christianity might very well increase in the world and bring a great number of individuals into submission to the laws of God—thus contributing to the ushering in of the "reign of Christ." The "postmillennialists" trust that this world evangelization will lead men and woman to experience a time of peace and prosperity, which in turn is the crowning and ultimate end of the "millennium." This optimistic framework has largely been adopted by the Roman Catholic Church and by several Protestant Churches in Europe, the United States, and Asia.

In countries with a Christian tradition, the "postmillennialists" favor tangible social progress, sometimes in hope of a broader sphere of influence. In general, they are well-disposed toward protecting the environment on behalf of their faith, although some defend more radical positions. For example, the proponents of "realized eschatology" or of "Christian socialism" in the nineteenth century gutted their Christian faith, so to speak, of all references to a transcendent God (and often to Christ the Redeemer), so as to promote "Christian" social activism in society. In the twentieth century, "liberation theology" took on a Marxist perspective in order to establish a world here and now where justice and social harmony reign patterned on the Christian (eschatological) hope.

One of the more recent developments of postmillennialism in Protestant and evangelical circles, especially in the United States, is the "Christian reconstruction" or "theonomy" movement. Its proponents highlight the influence of (authentic) Christian faith based on the law of God, which they believe to be on the rise in the social, cultural, and political life of the city. The reality is often rather different, or ambiguous at any rate.

Alas, even when committed or practicing Christians represent a significant proportion of the total population, they do not always exercise a profound and decisive—let alone good—influence on society, at least in the political and ecological arena.

Premillennialism

"Premillennialists" hold that the millennium is a thousand-year reign in a literal sense. It will be ushered in by Christ upon his return to earth following (or preceding, according to others) a period of natural and societal cataclysms, as well as an apostasy (renunciation of the Christian faith) on a massive scale. Some imagine then that this reign will be an era of regeneration for the earth, in part thanks to the good management of the people of God directed by Jesus Christ himself. If so, then what about the "new heavens and the new earth"?

Two main currents of thought stand out, according to which this "new creation" is placed before or after the millennium. But the proponents of these two positions do not always evince a keen interest in protecting the environment in the present day, before the return of Jesus Christ. Many believe, in effect, that the "former" earth will be completely destroyed and replaced by a radically new creation unrelated to the previous one. It is therefore not as important to be concerned about the preservation of this "first" creation. It is deemed necessary only to assure the optimal conditions of life for the maximum number of individuals (everyone, if possible!) on this terrestrial ball. Nonetheless, hope in the world to come outweighs, to a certain extent, present concerns. It is better to "preach the gospel," the good news of eternal salvation in Jesus Christ, than to "protect the environment" during this period preceding the millennium.

Obviously, we cannot minimize the prominent, indeed the preeminent place, reserved for the "missionary mandate," for it is surely more important "not to lose one's soul than to gain the world" (Matt. 16:26). However, we can advance at least three good reasons for countering the "fatalism" or ecological indifference that some-times characterizes premillennialists:

1. Care for creation is a form of respect and love toward God, its author. This attitude is analogous to that of the care one would certainly show to preserve the tableau of a grand master, such as Rembrandt or Monet, if one had in one's possession, in recognition of its artistic (and pecuniary!) value. What would be the reaction of the painter himself if he witnessed the degradation of his work, for want of care? Or if it were soiled or disfigured by the children of the house, who might have used it for their silly games?

2. The "end" (or the prelude to the end) does not justify in any way the lack of concern for this present life, for the protec-tion and preservation of creation, for the economic, social, scientific, and technological progress that even the most "ap-athetic" Christians nevertheless appreciate on a daily basis. We have already mentioned, on the other hand, that it is deemed normal to care for our body each day, although it is mortal; so the same applies to this world, even though we know it shall soon disappear.

3. Protecting the environment is also a way of loving one's neighbor who lives *within* this environment and depends *upon* this environment. This is true in every corner of the globe: no one can deny the benefit for the common good when one seeks, for example, to reduce automobile and in-dustrial pollution in Western cities or to restore the soils in developing countries.

In all events, we mainly have to remember that the "missionary mandate" does not nullify in any way the "cultural mandate." To be sure, the former gives the latter its fullest sense, since it fosters, at least in part, the reestablishment of the creation order in that the Lord is acknowledged and worshipped as the sole and ultimate king of cre-ation, the providential sovereign who actively sustains this world.

Amillennialism

"Amillennialists" believe that there is no millennium in the literal sense. Since this term, as they point out, appears in a symbolic book and in a symbolic context, it does not represent a "quantifiable" reality of a thousand years. Similar to "postmillennialists," they believe the "millennium" occurs during the first and the second coming of the Messiah. Unlike them, however, they do not await an extraordinary time at the end of this period, during which the Christian faith, linked to the acceptance of the gospel in the world, will reach its high point. For amillennialists, it is certainly important to declare throughout the entire world the good news of Christ crucified and resurrected, and they still hope that the acceptance of the gospel will be more widespread than ever. But the second coming of Jesus coincides with "the resurrection and the judgment of the living and the dead," ushering in the establishment of the unending reign of God over all creation delivered from evil, completely renewed by his power.

Generally speaking, Christian "amillennialists" are sensitive to the need for protecting the environment, for they tend to emphasize the continuity between the old creation and the new. They consider creation care to be a tangible sign of their faith in Jesus Christ, as well as their eschatological hope. They seem to manifest, however, the same deficiencies as the proponents of other positions, in particular when they neglect the "cultural mandate" or when they imagine that the new creation will be radically different from the old.

Lastly, the excesses of prosperity theology, which affects all Christian denominations just as it does the different eschatological theories, must be condemned here. This teaching claims that the divine blessing on Christians is manifested through financial prosperity, robust health, and success in every endeavor, including the numerical growth of believers in the life of the church. This triumphalist theology has often led to an unfortunate attitude of excessive domination over nature. It is fed by a very telling kind of greed when it comes to characterize some Christians who boast of their material blessings. It is often in this context that nature has been the most abused, for the sake of the unbridled enrichment of industrial farming and other developers. These "theologians" forget that in the list of "heroes of the faith," established in the Epistle to the Hebrews, are found men and women "deprived of everything," martyrs and other Christians abandoned amidst otherwise prosperous societies.

Moreover, this is to forget the teaching of Jesus who invites those who follow him to become servants in order to become better "masters," to renounce their riches in order to enrich their neighbors, not to fill their attics or their bank accounts more than necessary, but each day to count on God to receive from his hand their "daily bread."

The Balance Between Creation and Redemption

These three eschatological viewpoints present both strengths and weaknesses; yet more important than the exact time, nature, or timetable of the "millennium," it is striking the balance between the theology of creation and the theology of redemption that proves to be key.

If we insist on the theological importance of creation, then there is the danger of preaching a more "materialist" or earthbound gospel, with an emphasis on its "social" significance. In contrast, if we focus on redemption, there is the danger of "spiritualizing" the gospel or "disembodying" it, of emptying current life of its material reality and thus of neglecting the world and its resources. It is hence necessary to view creation and redemption through the same theological and eschatological prism.

In the final analysis, no one knows the day or the hour of the return of Jesus Christ, who shall be "seen by the entire earth" (Matt. 24:30). Meanwhile, care for creation in the present order, while at the same time nurturing a firm eschatological hope, is not always so simple.

The Future of Creation: Between
Discontinuity and Continuity

In a winsome extended metaphor, the prophet Isaiah paints the idyllic tableau of relationships transformed by the "shoot from the stump of Jesse," the Messiah upon whom "the Spirit of the LORD will rest":

> The wolf will live with the lamb, the leopard will lie down with the goat, the calf and the lion and the yearling together; and a little child will lead them. The cow will feed with the bear, their young will lie down together, and the lion will eat straw like the ox. The infant will play near the cobra's den, and the young child will put its hand into the viper's nest.
>
> (Isa. 11:5–8; see also Mic. 4:1–4)

The world of the future is described using categories from the present world order. We observe here that wild beasts lie in peace with domestic animals. In the Bible (and most often in nature), they are generally separated, both physically and symbolically. When the "wild beasts" (predators such as lions, or other dangerous animals such as serpents) invade the domain of men, they spread true terror. This state is one of the "curses" declared to be a consequence of the disobedience of the people of God to the commandments of the law, in particular when they give themselves over to idolatry (Lev. 26:22; Deut. 32:24; Hos. 2:4–15). But the reverse is also true: when faithful to the law, the people of God have nothing to fear from the "beasts of the field," who live then in their midst without causing harm to humans or to domestic herds. The Law of Moses provides even for wild animals to graze freely in fallow fields during a sabbatical year, after the poor and strangers have gleaned what they could once the owner has completed the harvest (Exod. 23:10–12). The prophet Isaiah announces then, with this exalted and colorful tableau, an era of reconciliation and peace, which is reflected in renewed relationships among living things. But it is obvious that this time has not yet come.

It bears remarking here an interesting aside made by Mark in his Gospel: Jesus "was in the wilderness forty days, being tempted by Satan. He was with the wild animals, and angels attended him" (Mark 1:13). The mention of wild beasts, whose behavior seems peaceful toward the Savior, appears to also be an eschatological sign of reconciliation with creation. We would do well to probe this biblical reflection concerning the place of "wild animals" in creation with a view to drawing out its "ecological implications."

For the time being, Christians live with varying degrees of success with this tension between the present and the future order. They know that the whole creation is called to salvation, to the reestablishment of all things. Right relations will be renewed between men and women, as well as with God, as both the apostles Peter and Paul mentioned in their sermons or letters (Acts 3:21; Rom. 8:18–23). Christians aim toward this end, but they take due note, not without chagrin, that they continue at times to forsake these new relations with God, with their neighbors, and with nature, in spite of their very best intentions. They nourish, however, the hope of one day seeing these relations perfectly reestablished when their Lord and Savior will appear once more to restore his visible reign throughout the entire universe, under new heavens and on a new earth.

While awaiting this felicitous denouement, what remains to be considered are the practicalities of safeguarding the present creation, also known as the "protection of the environment" or "nature."

7

FROM THEORY TO
PRACTICE

Human beings, whether they are Christians or not, are faced with a threefold challenge in the twenty-first century: to rethink their relationship with time, space, and natural resources. This challenge extends to a reexamination of the proper use of the unprecedented financial and technological means at their disposal for refashioning the environment and managing society. They are also challenged with evaluating—and adapting as a result—the manner in which they use resources to produce, process, and consume foodstuff and goods in general.

The production and consumption of energy poses in this sense a particular problem. Moreover, this new way of thinking and living in a more respectful orientation vis-à-vis the environment assumes a driving force. Now, it is not so easy to generate this driving force in societies where individuals display, if not reticence, at least a certain indifference when it comes to modifying their behavior so as to better preserve the environment on a local *and* planetary scale.

Christians find this driving force in their faith. They can thus confront the triple challenge of a different relationship with their environment from the perspective of the "kingdom of God," whether in this present age, including future generations of believers, or in the world to come at the second coming of Jesus Christ.

The ideal of a new relationship with time, space, and natural resources is laudable, but the practical reality is more complex, and at times contradictory.

Ecology and Economy

"Ecology," according to *Merriam-Webster's Dictionary*, is defined as that "branch of science concerned with the interrelationship of organisms and their environments," whereas "economy" is defined as "the structure or conditions of economic life in a country, area, or period."

An etymological link exists between the two terms, for both concern the management of the household (*oïkos*, from which derives the prefix *eco-*), and by extension the management of the city or the nation, if not all inhabited space (*oikoumenē*) or nature as a whole (see Matt. 24:14; Luke 21:36). This original sense of "economy" appears front and center in the first edition in 1828 of *Webster's Collegiate Dictionary*: "Primarily, the management, regulation and government of a family or the concerns of a household."

In the popular imagination, alas, ecology does not always rhyme with economy, and the semantic link that unites the two is weakened by the questionable—not to mention unstrained and irresponsible—behavior of human beings. How can we reconcile these two terms that are often considered antithetical?

Still, according to *Webster's* today, the term "economy" can signify as well the "thrifty and efficient use of material resources." It designates then the prudent and healthy practice of *limiting* expenses, without being given to greed or excessive cautiousness (too much saving can also pose problems!), so as to better manage personal, public, or natural assets. It is without doubt this last definition that allows us to find a common concept for reconciling "economy" and "ecology." And yet, do not the specialists of electrical production speak of "negawatts" to designate the energy not produced due to consumption savings? So, reconciliation of the two terms is not unheard of after all.

Economic Crisis and Ecological Crisis

It is unfortunate that wealthy countries tend to need a major economic crisis to goad them into acting in a "thrifty and efficient" manner. To be sure, the proper management of goods, whether in family-owned businesses or entrusted to state administrators, should imply not only long-range planning and economic development but also measures for garnering savings or at least avoiding waste.

The Bible tells the story of Joseph who, when he was prime minister to the Egyptian Pharaoh (second millennium BC), had reserves built up in a period of plenty to prepare for the ensuing years of want. Why should we then be surprised that crises arise on a regular basis? Economic cycles, more or less widespread and frequent, punctuate the life of every human society. They have been described and analyzed by numerous economists for centuries.

The leaders of society, as well as the on-the-go consumers that we too often are, could actually draw inspiration from this example of Joseph in ancient Egypt. That would help us, for instance, to avoid jumping on the bandwagon of the hawkers of goods and loans that are too good to be true. For it was precisely these risky speculations and acrobatic financial arrangements, most notably in the United States, that in 2008 sparked (or amplified) a large-scale world economic crisis. In the background of this was the energy crisis, which was linked to the price of oil and whose jagged fluctuations had been disrupting the global economic system since the 1970s. It was as if the Goddess of Greed bit the hand of her worshipers (i.e., those all-too-greedy bankers and lending institutions) and her willing slaves (i.e., those reckless borrowers), who drew the entire world into a downward spiral that especially weakened the poorest and the most vulnerable. The negative spillover effects of such behavior on the environment are significant.

More recently, it has suddenly dawned on the ruling class, as if caught unawares, that developed countries are being undermined by a colossal domestic debt that dangles the prospect of national bankruptcy over the head of each and every citizen. In France in 2019, public debt (state, social security, regional authorities) reached nearly 100% of the gross domestic product (GDP), or almost 2,400 billion euros (more than 32,000 euros per inhabitant), and it increases by about 2,500 euros *per second*. The situation is much more alarming in Japan (234% of GDP), followed in Europe by Greece (178% of GDP) and Italy (131% of GDP). The average debt in Europe has now climbed to 81.5%. The United States (105% of GDP) alone accrues to itself a third of the world's pubic debt—more than 20 trillion dollars as of 2017 (it increases by $45,000 per second and represents $78,000 per inhabitant). Along with Japan and China, the accumulated debt of these three states represents 50% of the debt. The costs of financing this debt are being reduced, in particular thanks to very low borrowing rates, but there are questions about the duration of this trompe l'oeil upturn. As of spring 2020, everything is now being called into question by the crisis caused by the Covid-19 pandemic.

The situation is all the more worrisome in that the public debt of some populous "emerging" nations—those with recent development such as Brazil and India—increases continually. In "low income" countries (roughly 20% of the world population), the average public debt has reached 45% (14% more between 2013 and 2017). Some highly indebted poor nations (HIPC, 36 states in total) have seen their debt reduced and sometimes forgiven entirely; however, without resulting in any change with respect to their financial situation, which remains alarming. It is estimated today that the accumulated world debt of nations, businesses, and households has climbed to 237 trillion dollars. Some continue to predict, in spite of the rise of overall GDP, a major worldwide crash.[1] While new financial safeguards have been issued and regulations applied on various levels, will they be sufficient?

Public debt built up over the years when developed or rapidly developing countries were swept up by the postwar wave of prosperity—the "Glorious Thirty"[2]—whose declining momentum

---

[1] See the site l'IIF (Institute of International Finance), https://www.iif .com/publications/global-debt-monitor and the "clocks" or "counters" of public debt, http://www.dettepublique.fr/ et http://www.theusdebtclock .com/.

[2] This refers in France to the thirty-year boom following World War II.—Trans.

some have not been able (or did not want?) to notice, rocked as they were on several occasions since 1973 by oil price hikes. During the years of plenty, like Joseph, it would have been better practice to build up reserves, set limits, and build safeguards (alas, those needing to be "guarded" in the world of economic trade are legion) against the excesses of the financial system, which is often fueled by the unbridled greed of its most opportunistic and unscrupulous agents.

Power and Wealth, Production and Consumption

At this very time, an entire chemical and technological arsenal—fine-tuned to master time, space, and resources—was unleashed without restraint. Admittedly, this unleashing was in large part necessary for want of a better solution (and in ignorance of the consequences) to meet an unprecedented demographic challenge. Let us not therefore pass judgment too hastily on those who preceded us and who may have made mistakes, for we do not know what might have been our own response in similar circumstances. But it is imperative that we draw lessons from our history, so as to respond accordingly. It is becoming increasingly clear that this poorly planned period of growth has had dramatic consequences on society and that for too long a blind eye has been turned to the production, processing, sale, and use of products now deemed hazardous to humans and the environment without taking proper countermeasures.

Among the consequences in question: accidents resulting from the over-exploration of natural resources (petroleum leads the list) have proliferated; industrialization has at times appeared uncontrolled; the frantic consumerism of humans has become one of the inveterate traits of developed nations, where there is now an increasing proportion of obese children and adults—or contrariwise, a whole set of diet enthusiasts slimming down in all sorts of outlandish ways! "Their god is their belly," wrote the apostle Paul to the Philippians to condemn those Christians not living consistently with their faith, who were interested only in the material things of this world (Phil. 3:19). It is now known today that excess weight, coupled with lack of physical activity, is a cause of premature death just as worrisome as pollution or some epidemics.

We are now caught up in a system, which is far from virtuous, for making many of the objects we use, starting with the most necessary ones such as our clothes, even the most "ecological" ones. Before we could dress up, for example, with a T-shirt made of cotton (100%!), we had to plant the cotton, grow it, harvest it, process it, transport it to the points of sale, and then get it to the user. This required seeds, water, manpower, machinery, and a mechanical and chemical industry (weaving, dyeing, etc.), means of transport (boats, planes, trucks, cars, etc.), and a shopping area, generally in urban areas. For "natural" reasons (cotton does not grow everywhere) and economic reasons (labor costs, industrial specialization, etc.), this garment is the product of a system that can be extended to the whole world. In the end, the "carbon balance" of this product, although elementary, remains high, even if we try to reduce it by all means, which is never simple. If we then add synthetic fibers that are derived from oil, the problem becomes even more complicated.

Consumers have gotten into the habit of discarding goods after a single use, the shelf life of which is often even preprogrammed by manufacturers in quest of a good return on their investment! Some were sentenced to heavy fines following the lawsuits brought against them for this reason. Nowadays, in any case, it is undeniable that most household appliances or electronics are conceived and manufactured for a rather short operating time. Many items are also next to impossible to repair, not because of the technical difficulty but in large part because of the labor costs. This short-term turnover of products is made all the easier due to the financial wherewithal (i.e., quick credit) of consumers. The use of computers and cell phones, a many-headed Hydra according to numerous studies, is a perfect example. In any case, both the manufacture and the disposal of these greatly desired and otherwise highly effective information and communication tools pose a number of problems for society. Yet these problems are merely being offloaded to poor countries—without Western consciences being troubled in the slightest, or so it seems.

It is now entirely conceivable that human beings themselves, since they are judged less productive beyond the age of 50, might be deemed "disposable." The temptation of speed, as when driving a car, plays a major role in the electronics field, with a major consequence on energy consumption and therefore also its production. The announced implementation of a "5G" network in many countries poses various problems in this respect. This equipment uses three times more energy than the "4G" network and involves three times as many sites to ensure coverage deemed sufficient. In the end, this would represent an increase in electricity consumption (around 2%?). It would also be necessary to add to this balance sheet the manufacture of the necessary elements, especially the replacement of telephones for this new network. Is it really useful? For whom in particular—companies, individuals? For what gain in time and efficiency? With what impact on the environment? What about the budgets of families (and the inequalities this can generate) and businesses? We must think before we act. How can this sad state of affairs possibly be reversed, either in the private or the public sector?

The Role of Political Bodies

Any "ecological" steps taken by individuals or families— together they add up—can have an overall positive impact on the environment. These minor measures provide an opportunity to reconsider on an often crucial small scale our relationship with time, space, and natural resources. More often than not, though, for meaningful change to occur, it is necessary to appeal to the authority of governing bodies, in theory elected by a majority of citizens, at least in a democratic system.

If, for example, we wish to conserve fuel (our relationship with natural resources), it might be necessary to rediscover the benefits of bicycling—as long as safe and secure bike paths can be laid out. On an individual level, if this new mode of transportation involves a slower commute than by car, travel time will have to be reassessed (our relationship with time). With biking, for those with a busy downtown commute, it may be possible to actually gain time! In any event, elected officials and high-level business leaders have a definite role to play in the organization of space and the layout of traffic systems (our relationship with space).

To be sure, choices are not always easy to make, both individually and collectively. The constraints—whether natural (topography), familial (number of children, for example), personal (inability to use a bicycle for whatever reason, including arriving at work drenched in sweat), or the distance between home and the workplace, and so on—are not so simple to overcome. And if cyclists are few in number, then the use of this means of transportation in the midst of a sea of cars could have disastrous effects on the nerves, not to mention health. It is therefore incumbent to think on a city-wide, regional, national or even global scale.

From the perspective of public officials, some measures can make their heads spin. If overnight, every city dweller abandoned their car for a bicycle—which some advocate and strongly militate for—then their entire national and international economic system stands the risk of severe interruption. Indeed, the automobile remains a common consumer good. The major automobile industries support a host of workers and subcontractors, so an overly abrupt disruption would be the death knell signaling certain unemployment and bankruptcy.

It is easy to understand, then, the awkwardness and hesitation of political officials when it comes to taking "ecological" measures. It has also not been established whether drivers would be readily willing to give up their cars. Alas, the paucity of bikers now riding in cities— where topography is not an issue, bike lanes have been laid out, and even showers installed in businesses and government buildings—is ample proof that there is a lack of interest, to say the least. Only the Dutch, who benefit from a flat terrain and who manage to brave the most unfavorable weather conditions, have been successful in opting for bike travel whether in the city or the countryside.[3]

---

[3] On this point, see Frédéric Héran, *Le retour de la bicyclette, Une histoire des déplacements urbains en Europe de 1817 à 2050* (Paris: La Dé-

In order to create an environment accessible to human beings in optimal conditions and protected from external hazards, it would be necessary to set aside an entire non-car-dependent space. This would entail a total modification of urban planning designs so as to lessen as much as possible travel between various poles of activity—business, leisure, and personal residence. But is this even possible? History enshrined in the collective conscience cannot be rewritten, for it would be too daunting to rearrange the spaces of settlements shaped by populations over the centuries. However, we can still dream of more autonomous neighborhoods, where one day homes, schools, recreation centers, businesses, and workplaces will be found in proximity. Although we can settle for less grandiose schemes, we have to wonder whether they will be adopted willingly or applied by force.

Authority and Power

A number of ecological movements and their leaders now encourage political bodies to impose environmental laws by degree. Our democracies exercise caution, and rightly so, with respect to coercive measures. Some believe, then, that proactive measures such as increasing fuel prices would spur drivers to find other means of transportation, such as mass transit, which is less costly and cleaner.

When a Parisian couple, however, was recently asked how their weekend travel plans might change if gas prices were lowered, they responded with brutal candor, "We'd drive more . . ." In the realm of transportation, to be sure, a positive outcome seems out of reach for the French, if we judge merely by the ever-increasing flow of automobiles during winter and summer holidays, or simply on

---

couverte, 2014). The author describes the recent development of cycle transportation in large European cities. Moreover, he demonstrates that reduced speed limits in urban centers (recommended at 30 km/h) and appropriate infrastructure (bicycle lanes) favor the safety of cyclists and have as a byproduct the immediate increase in bicycle transportation.

weekends, not to mention during daily commutes—and this is in spite of significant overall increases in fuel costs over the past few years. These measures are also highly unpopular, for they impinge upon the sacrosanct "purchasing power" of consumers.

The civic-minded are few and far between who would accept, if not willingly at least with a certain resignation, any diminishment in their standard of living during a period of crisis. Consumers hunker down over their "acquired advantages," without ever considering a crisis to be the consequence of both an individual *and* collective "failure." Each individual tends to believe that no one is really to blame, or else that it is only "those other people" who are in the wrong!

It would be a welcome sign of "repentance," after all, if there was both a personal and collective acknowledgement of responsibility; but this term now seems old-fashioned, even reactionary, in our post-Christian societies. On that account, it would not be any better to resort to guilt-tripping, as is the wont of some irresponsible and mischievous agitators who wish only to lord it over their fellow citizens. In the final instance, it must be admitted that for political authorities, any economic downturn is a great challenge to manage.

Let us imagine that our authorities, pressed by the urgent need to reduce greenhouse gases to halt global warming, suddenly decide to stop using fossil fuels altogether. We have already mentioned the economic consequences that such a radical measure could have, for example, for the automobile industry. This time, however, we need to think more broadly. It is in fact society as a whole that would be at risk, on all scales. Transport, most of which is highly dependent on oil, would rapidly diminish or cease; oil-heated homes would cool down just as quickly; in large cities, where most people and activities (industries and services) are concentrated, the daily supply of all kinds of products, especially food, would be disrupted from day one. Such a sudden change would quickly cause panic. After the first few days of survival, thanks to the food reserves, the situation would become anarchic and violent, with everyone trying to survive, this time by any means. The best structured and balanced democracy would probably not be able to withstand it. And if we consider the dependence of our societies on electrical energy, which is only partly supplied by nuclear power stations in the world, it is even easier to imagine the disorder and the human and material damage such a shutdown could cause. In order to reduce the risks, it is therefore recommended to adopt a more gradual reduction (or transition) policy, constantly seeking the best compromise between economic requirements and ecological imperatives. This is what the specialists, scientists, economists, and senior officials of the "Club of Rome" have been advocating for over fifty years. But this does not sit well with the most "extremist" people on either side. What will be the attitude of the authorities, tossed between the imperatives of economic and ecological survival?

Should, then, the virtues of "downsizing" be extoled, as the notion has been understood since the establishment of the "Club of Rome" in the 1960s? This was when intimidating warnings were issued with respect to the demographic, economic, and ecological threats looming on the horizon, all of which were clearly and yet mysteriously interconnected. English economist Malthus would never have imagined in his time of the early nineteenth century that a population of over seven billion people could derive its subsistence (yet poorly distributed, alas) from this terrestrial ball. Nevertheless, it would appear that it might be possible to feed an even greater population, provided that they can be satisfied with living within more reasonable parameters of comfort, resource use, and energy consumption throughout the the world. Let us recall here that growth, at least numerically, was posed as an "order" by God in the beginning. Should it be questioned? It remains to be seen what is the appropriate balance between the authority imposed from above by politicians and the goodwill conceded by the population with intelligence and wisdom: the problem now concerns, no doubt to varying degrees, all societies in the world.

The Ecological Debate on a Planetary Scale

Environmental issues have now become international in scope. Over the past thirty years, practical solutions have been sought on a planetary scale to reduce the negative impact of human activity on nature.

In the nineteenth century, a handful of idealists with naturalist, philanthropic, or aesthetic aims had already found a way to make their voices heard. In Europe and in North America, swept up by the Romantic Movement and the rise of natural sciences that paid new attention to "nature," they did what they could to protect wildlife from further infringement on their domain or cruel and overly commercial exploitation. They endeavored to preserve rural areas, to defend the quality of life as it was then threatened by the expansion of large industrial cities. They are responsible as well for the establishment of national parks such as Yellowstone in 1872, in the United States and the National Trust for Places of Historic Interest or Natural Beauty in Great Britain in 1895.

It is also thanks to their efforts, soon seconded by a growing cadre of activists in international organizations, such as the International Office for the Protection of Nature (IOPN) founded in Brussels in 1928, that legislation was strengthened to protect birdlife, forests, or nature in the broad sense. But the tangible impact of these measures was hampered by economic challenges and by political setbacks as a result of major world conflicts. Their impact has also been limited by the demographic explosion, advances in industrial civilization, and the strong desire of populations to see their standard of living improve. The advocates for nature were often, therefore, taken for sweet dreamers.

Scientific Assessment

Since the middle of the twentieth century, ecological questions have come more into focus in public discussions. At the end of the Second World War, nations became brutally aware of the power of nuclear weapons. For the first time in history, a single bomb could destroy every living creature over a land mass and to an extent never before imagined. The radiation effects of an atomic explosion also remain much longer than those of classical warfare, continuing to wreak biological havoc long afterward. Doomsday weaponry has rapidly proliferated, even though attempts have been made to limit their production by limiting them to certain hegemonic rivals, whom, it may be hoped, are still reasonable.

As early as the 1950s, on a large scale and in a more substantial way, populations began to suffer from the consequences of pollution due to the commercial exploitation of natural resources. At an initial stage, reactions against this rapidly deteriorating situation remained few and far between.

In 1962 in the United States, Rachel Carson published her work *Silent Spring*, which constituted a turning point in the history of modern ecology. She studied in particular the measurable consequences of the spread of DDT in the environment (the use of this product was prohibited in 1972 in the United States) and provides an uncompromising assessment: "To have risked so much in our efforts to mold nature to our satisfaction and yet to have failed in achieving our goal would indeed be the final irony. Yet this, it seems, is our situation."[4] She is not, however, alone in vigorous condemnation with undeniable scientific evidence in support of the damage caused by the abusive use of the veritable chemical arsenal available to farmers for pest control and to reduce weed infestations in crops.

Across the Atlantic, the novel *Les racines du ciel* by Frenchman Romain Gary, who denounces in his particular literary manner (as emblematic of a larger context) the massacre of elephants in Africa, won the Prix Goncourt in 1956.[5] His work has often been hailed as the first ecological novel, for it issues "the first distress call with respect to our threatened biosphere." Yet in the preface to the 1980 edition, the author avers that he did not fully appreciate initially "the extent of the destruction being perpetrated or the magnitude of the peril." He adds, "Ecological awareness itself has to face what I would call man's inhumanity to man."[6]

---

[4] Rachel Carson, *Silent Spring* (Boston: Houghton Mifflin, 1962), 245.

[5] Romain Gary's novel was soon translated and published in English as *The Roots of Heaven* (New York: Simon and Schuster, 1958).—Trans.

[6] Ibid., preface.

As stated in chapter 4, Jean Dorst also contributed in France to the awareness of the deterioration of the environment. One of the first to publish a scientific work on the state of the planet, he meticulously documented his work and made it accessible to the general public.[7] Today, the alarm has finally been sounded to an even greater extent by the media, of course, and it now seems to be taken seriously.

Political Action

But it was René Dumont in the 1970s who brought ecology to the fore of French political discussion. In 1974, he garnered 1.3% of the votes in the presidential election. Environment candidates then went on to capture 3.8% of votes cast (Brice Lalonde in 1981 and Antoine Waechter in 1995), but they peaked at 5.25% with Noël Mamère in 2002, only to fall back to 1.57% in 2007 with Dominique Voynet and 2.32% in 2012 with Eva Joly. Before the 2017 election, the environmental candidate (EELV) Yannick Jadot endorsed the socialist candidate Benoît Hamon. The results have been essentially the same (between 2% and 7%) in legislative elections. On the other hand, the environment tickets obtained higher scores (among French voters) in European Parliamentary elections: about 7% of votes cast in 1984, 10.6% in 1989, and reaching as high as 16.3% in 2009. In 2014, however, the decline is precipitous with only 8.95% in total (the "Greens" represent 6.6% of the deputies in the European Parliament).

These figures suggest that on a national level, French voters believe ecology should be integrated into the platforms of the different political parties. When it comes to the European Parliament, environmental concerns make themselves more palpably felt, in part probably as a protest vote, in a venue where the usual political

---

[7] Jean Dorst, *Avant que nature meure. Pour une écologie politique*, 6th ed., revised and enlarged (Neuchâtel: Delachaux et Niestlé, 1978). More recently, recognized scientists such as Jean-Marie Pelt have been able to disseminate their works with a view to building awareness among as wide a public as possible.

and human stakes are without doubt more muddled and further removed. It is finally noteworthy here that the erosion of the communist Left has essentially been to the benefit of "Green" parties.

It is now recognized in Europe, among politicians of every stripe, that ecology should play a part in policymaking. Indeed, administrations now systematically include a department dedicated to ecology, the environment, and/or sustainable development, though sometimes it is combined with energy and transportation. In 2017, the French government created a department called the Ministry for the Ecological and Solidary Transition. According to a decree promulgated on May 24, 2017, this department is charged with preparing and implementing the government's policy in the following domains:

> Sustainable development; environment, including protection and enhancement of nature and biodiversity; green technologies; energy transition and energy, especially with respect to tariffs; climate; prevention of natural and technological risks; industrial safety; transport and their infrastructure; equipment and the sea; battle against global warming and atmospheric pollution; sustainable management of scarce resources.

Ecology has thus become a discipline in its own right, recognized and studied in universities. It has also now turned into an ideological movement, with its own well-defined political platform, whose goals are obviously more controversial when tainted by counterculture bohemianism, revolutionary thought, or New Age spirituality—and now "alter-globalization" (or "alternative globalization" or "altermondialism"). But the entire planet has now woken up: the threat is seen as planetary, and solutions must be proposed *for* and *by* all the inhabitants of the earth.

The Great International Conferences

International conferences organized around the topic of environmental protection began with the 1972 United Nations summit

"Only One Earth" held in Stockholm. The United Nations Environment Program (UNEP) was established that same year, with a view
to strengthening and coordinating public and private initiatives for
the protection of the environment on a worldwide level.

A number of ecological disasters had a role thereafter in awak-
ening consciences in wealthy nations, previously carried away by
the euphoria of several decades of economic expansion and relative
abundance. They served to influence world opinion concerning the
dangers of poorly managed development and the attendant risks
of pollution. But economic interests remain uppermost in most
minds, often to the detriment of ecological imperatives and the
preservation of natural resources in the medium and long term.

In crisis situations, however, political authorities have begun
to take effective measures to reign in the various industrial opera-
tions considered most precarious and most polluting. Such was the
case, for example, when a "hole" was discovered in the stratospheric
ozone layer that shields life here on earth by absorbing most ultra-
violet rays. The international community reacted and prohibited
fairly quickly, as early as 1979 in America and in northern Europe,
the use of fluorinated hydrocarbons (CFC) either in gaseous or
liquid form, which is responsible for the deterioration of the strato-
sphere (at an altitude of between 10 and 50 kilometers). This alarming situation led the international delegates, who were meeting in
Geneva, to take a closer look at climate change in collaboration
with the World Meteorological Organization (WMO) created in
1947. The number of meetings has only multiplied around the world.

In 1992, the Rio de Janeiro summit marked an important milestone when it brought together heads of state or government delegates from a majority of countries in the world. The result was
the drafting of a *Framework Convention on Climate Change*, now
signed by nearly 200 countries. Other communiqués issuing from
the summit concern more specifically the call for preservation of
biodiversity.

The outcome of the World Summit on Sustainable Development, held in Johannesburg in 2002 and again in Rio in 2012, might
be judged positively when considering the texts that were drafted

and agreed to upon these occasions. But, unfortunately, these summits turned out to be disappointing given the reluctance and challenges in actually implementing these treatises.

Beginning in 1995, an annual meeting called the Conference of the Parties (COP) has brought together representatives of the signatory states of the 1992 Convention, as well as delegates from local governments, countless NGOs, private firms, civilian society, and so on.

In Johannesburg in 2002, the Kyoto Protocol, drawn up in 1997 (COP 3), was approved by all the states present. The protocol called on some forty industrialized countries to reduce emissions of six (or seven) greenhouse gases (GHG; essentially carbon dioxide and methane) by at least 5% between 2008 and 2012, based on a baseline reached in 1990. These gases contribute to increasing *natural* greenhouse gases (necessary for maintaining the average earth temperature at a viable level for living organisms), and they contribute to "climate change," which is measured today by scientists with more accuracy. The broad consensus among the scientific community is that change is in large part linked to human activity over the course of the past two centuries (which especially saw an increase in carbon monoxide as a result of deforestation, energy production, industrialization, transportation, construction, etc.). In February 2005, the Kyoto Protocol went into effect thanks to the ratification *in extremis* by Russia in November 2004, which helped make the quorum of 55 countries emitting at least 55% of greenhouse gases. It has now been ratified by those states that had made a commitment in Johannesburg in 2002, with the notable exception of the United States, which in turn somewhat weakens the protocol's symbolic weight and practical authority.

The Paris Conference in 2015 (COP 21) aimed at finalizing the agreement for reducing greenhouse gases so as to limit global warming to a maximum of 2°C, compared to levels reached before the Industrial Revolution (circa 1780), even down to 1.5°C if possible. On November 4, 2016, the Paris Climate Agreement went into effect. It was again ratified by some 55 countries emitting at least 55% of the greenhouse gases, including China (22.4% in 2012), the United States (12.2%), the European Union (8.7%), India (6.1%), Russia (4.7%), Indonesia (4.2%), and Brazil (3.8 %). In all, 168 countries ratified the agreement.[8]

The agreement has, however, been criticized for remaining vague on the timeframe for capping emissions (in principle, 2020 would be the milestone year). These emissions are also difficult to track with precision due to the variety of heat-trapping gases, their lifetime in the atmosphere, and their relative disruptiveness.[9] The methods employed for controlling them is a matter of ongoing debate: reduction in the consumption of fossil fuel, CO_2 capture (reforestation), and so on. The flexibility left to states to set their own objectives in accordance with their means has been criticized. The difficulty in containing warming to 1.5°C is also frequently pointed out. It was estimated in 2016, for instance, that the average temperature of the earth had increased by 1.1 C compared to the preindustrial era. Moreover, the years 2015 to 2017 were the hottest ever recorded. The objective of limiting warming to 2°C by the end of the twenty-first century therefore seems increasingly compromised. As a result, some have called for a tighter check on the financial aid granted to developing nations within the framework of the agreement so as to prevent these undesirable effects.

More recently, the COP 23—which was held in Bonn, Germany, in November 2017 under the chairmanship of the Fiji Islands (on behalf of small island nations threatened by rising seas as a result of warming)—was marred by the official withdrawal of the United States from the Paris Climate Agreement just announced on June 1

---

[8] Official documents of these meeting are accessible of the United Nations site: https://unfccc.int/documents. For the Paris Climate Agreement, see https://unfccc.int/process-and-meetings/the-paris-agreement/ the-paris-agreement.

[9] Presently, the "Global Warming Potential" (GWP) of a GHG is calculated based on that of a quantity of CO_2, which is the ratio between the energy reflected toward the earth over 100 years per 1 kg of CO_2 and that which would be reflected by 1 kg of a GHG. The period covered, the quantity, and the lifetime of the different greenhouse gases would thus be at issue.

the same year. The COP 24 in Katowice (Poland) in 2018 and COP 25 in Madrid (Spain) in 2019, if they are allowed to adopt a Practical Handbook to implement the 2015 resolutions, were judged to be not very fruitful and even for some likely to discourage countries moderately motivated by the "ecological transition," which was nonetheless deemed necessary.

The United States and Ecology

American reticence in response to the ecological measures approved by the majority of nations had already been an issue during the Hague Conference in November 2000. George W. Bush, the recently elected president of the United States at the time—thanks in part to votes cast by conservative evangelical Christians—announced as early as March 2001 his unwillingness to ratify the accord, which otherwise he supported for ethical reasons. To justify this contradiction, he raised the usual specter of job loss should these measures be passed.

In 2002, the United States thus put into place their own protocol for greenhouse gas reduction, which was more modest and certainly less restrictive and a far cry from the requirements intended for the international community and especially for North America. Nevertheless, several factors contributed to significantly easing the misgivings of American policymakers and the public at large. These include the ecological measures taken by some progressive states such as California and Massachusetts, the election in 2008 of Barak Obama and his reelection in 2012—seen as more favorable to a policy that takes into account environmental concerns—and, lastly, the great 2008 financial crisis stemming from the excesses of an abusive economic system.

Since 2005, the debate has been rejoined as a result of shale gas exploration. Should the exploration of this new energy market be pursued and developed with the same technological methods (hydraulic fraction) that consume vast quantities of water and that have been deemed hazardous for the environment, since they pollute water tables? From a strictly economic standpoint and in view of the present lifestyle conditions of an average American (or European), the answer seems to be "full steam ahead." The central question remains whether it is still possible to reduce energy consumption, especially oil and gas. Even so, there is a need to clarify by which means this reduction might be achieved and what should be its underlying motivation. Among the unintended and yet positive consequences of shale gas exploration, it is important to note the decline of CO_2 emissions because of the decrease in coal mining and combustion, notably for power generation.

More recently, the election of Donald Trump as president has once again turned the American position on its head with respect to the measures taken by the international community in attempting to reign in global warming. Following the administration's withdrawal from the Paris Agreement in 2017, which would have gone into effect in 2020 under existing rules, several American states—encouraged by private companies and well-known figures among the commercial and celebrity class—have taken legal measures to counter this decision. Their stand thus constitutes an implicit critique of the "climate skepticism" commonly displayed in the United States. They pledge to reduce in a meaningful way—often beyond international requirements—their greenhouse gas emissions and, by the same token, to favor the use of renewable biofuels and energies. On that score, the states of New York and California committed in 2017 to reducing carbon emissions by 80% over a period of 60 years (1990 to 2050) and to using 50% renewable energies by 2030.

Emerging Nations

Some countries such as China, India, and Brazil have worked out a way to delve gradually into the Kyoto process without curbing their industrial development. It is well known, however, that China and India lead the list of energy-consuming nations and that they emit large quantities of the six main heat-trapping gases, in particular carbon dioxide. This is likewise the case for major oil-exporting nations, whose impact on the environment, relative to their small populations, is considerable. China claims to have committed itself with resolve to emission reductions, at the same time as it develops renewable energies—the only way for its urban population to escape asphyxiation.

Nevertheless, according to estimates, it would be necessary to reduce emissions by at least 60% on a worldwide basis to stabilize the current situation. How do we grapple with these depressing figures? What is all the more disconcerting is that climate-change inertia can be compared to that of a heavy piece of machinery set in motion at a high speed: any slowdown or change in direction is delicate and requires a lot of maneuvering; unwanted molecules, such as CO_2, emitted on this very day, will not disappear for a century.

International Perspectives

The recommendations put forward during the international colloquium held in Dakar, Senegal, back in March 2002 "Francophonie and Sustainable Development" (*What are the Issues, the Priorities for a 2012 Timeline?*), are still very much relevant today, as they were intended to be. They encapsulate quite accurately the commonly proposed environmental guidelines both on an international as well as a local basis:

- Promote multiculturalism within the framework of sustainable development;
- Increase environmental education and awareness as well as scientific cooperation, especially in research and in particular as it relates to clean water;
- Assure better dissemination of information;
- Change the economic paradigm and rethink production patterns;
- Focus on the human sphere as a whole rather than on the individual;

- Take into account the adaption efforts of the poorest nations, in particular those in Africa;
- Strengthen international law jurisdiction and work for a form of world governance.[10]

If these proposed measures seem proactive and self-evident, and if they are even followed to a certain extent in many nations, their limitations cannot help but come immediately to the fore. The countries most affected by the recommendations of global summits drag their feet to ratify the agreements or to comply with the guidelines that result from them. The leviathan of the economy as well as the standard of living or modes of production of wealthy nations—the most energy consuming—continue to trump the basic needs of a large swath of humanity. Is it right to prioritize the "human sphere" in the abstract when all behavioral change begins, as is well known, on an individual basis, and since the individual deserves to be respected, with his own rights? Lastly, with respect to the strengthening of international law and especially world governance, whose controlling authority remains ambiguous, is there not a risk of establishing a form of "environmental tyranny"?

Mere Window-Dressing Measures

Broad is the consensus nowadays that measures must be taken to preserve the environment and reduce greenhouse gas emissions. The recommendations expressed by the Grenelle Environment Forum in France in 2007, or more recently those formulated in conformity with the Paris Climate Agreement in 2015, center on this very point and add their voice to the chorus for significant behavioral change. But are these repeated alarms and the measures proposed by various political parties in power sufficient to raise, beyond a mere recognition of the challenges at issue, a genuine will to modify consumer behavior to counteract the ecological crisis?

---

[10] See www.sommetjohannesburg.org/initiatives/rapfinal-dakar.htm.

There is a risk in settling for "ecofriendly measures," which may ease the conscience but which serve only to allow individuals to continue living, in real terms, in the same manner. In the public and private sphere, advice is omnipresent for encouraging environmental preservation: turn off the faucet when brushing teeth, turn off unnecessary lights, eschew showers in favor of baths, insulate houses, reduce car travel, recycle waste, and so on. While all of these measures are worthwhile and impactful, considering as well that they have an even greater impact when multiplied on a total population-wide scale, they remain superficial *in substance*— seeming to excuse individuals from adopting a new lifestyle that is more in keeping with the true *limitations* of the planet, the living organisms that inhabit it, and natural resources. Although well intentioned, these measures seem to be mere window-dressing measures, limited to the narrow dimension of human beings focused on their do-goodism.

Ecological Contradictions

Thus, when the rubber hits the road, the practical application of measures conceived in the abstract is another story. These measures might appear utopian, if not hopeless, for some consider the small gestures recommended for protecting the environment to be lost in a sea of ecological challenges. Others raise, and rightly so, the numerous contradictions of some measures or at least their "negative" aspects. They often deem them poorly targeted. Still others underscore the great naïveté with which ecological questions are approached, thereby creating confusion in the minds of consumers often ill-informed or overwhelmed by a mass of sometimes conflicting information, if not manipulated with an obvious ideological bent or mercantile intent. The excesses are all the more sensitive as the multiplication of "fake news" and lies of all kinds circulating on social networks (and feeding many conspiracy theories) makes it even more difficult to discern between what could be considered "good" or "bad." The confusion and contradictions it creates do not make the task easy for authorities and consumers alike. We will provide two examples here of this naïveté with respect to energy consumption.

Low-Energy Bulbs

Should society impose upon the entire population, to take one example, the use of "low-energy" fluorescent lightbulbs? Such is already the case in France. Since January 1, 2013, conventional incandescent lightbulbs have no longer been available for sale. The electricity savings are real (three to four times less energy consuming than conventional bulbs), similarly in financial terms (with a savings of about 50 euros a year per household), despite the high price of these new bulbs (they are roughly five times more expensive than conventional bulbs, though their service life is longer).

At least four "drawbacks" to this "mandate" can be cited (and, indeed, are often mentioned according to popular opinion):

1. *Manufacturing and recycling.* In production, low-energy bulbs require more materials than conventional bulbs, especially "rare earths" (fluorescent powders produced mainly in China), gaseous mercury (from 3 mg to 25 mg depending on the model), plastic (an oil product), and various components for the electronic board. Although these new bulbs are 97% reusable, their cost is higher than that of incandescent bulbs (due to the different materials used in production), and only 35% to 40% of these bulbs are currently brought to collection points by users.

2. *Health and environmental issues.* The gaseous mercury present in bulbs is dangerous if they are broken by the user and then picked up without care (contact with the skin or released into the air, especially if a vacuum cleaner is employed to remove the debris). Gaseous mercury is toxic (more so than metallic mercury). If these bulbs are not recycled in the appropriate system, this gas can spread into the environ-

ment. Moreover, it is also the case that these bulbs, when turned on, produce ultraviolent and electromagnetic radiation (at a distance of 20 cm to 30 cm, perhaps even more)— radio frequencies that are suspected of having significant effects on humans (though this remains to be confirmed, and it might very well be that the real effect is null).

3. *A forced approach.* The consumer has not been given a choice of any possible alternative, at least at the onset. Now, it has not even been determined yet that the financial savings are assured, in part because the service life of these bulbs, purported to be 7,500 hours on average, has often proven to be inferior to that indicated on the packaging (this is the case for as many as 70% of bulbs). Other types of bulbs have now been proposed, in particular LED (light-emitting diode) bulbs that are more energy efficient (though still expensive) and notably less hazardous for the user than fluorescent lamps. Their use is trending these days, while fluorescent bulbs have gradually disappeared from the shelves. However, LED bulbs have disadvantages in terms of manufacturing (rare materials) and recycling, but solutions are emerging to resolve them gradually, at least in part.

4. *A lower priority objective.* Electric energy consumption on domestic lighting represents merely 2% to 3% of total consumption, and it represents between 8% and 15% (depending on electrical use for heating or hot water) of the average electricity bill of households. Appliances, such as the refrigerator or the freezer, are much more energy consuming. It is more efficacious, then, to concentrate efforts on these appliances, not to mention the truly behemoth consumers such as industry. The example applies as well to water usage, which households have been encouraged to economize while agriculture consumes about 70% of this resource. It is more advantageous to send well-trained engineers to advise farmers and help them reduce consumption.

Electric Cars

Some individuals like to pat themselves on the back for taking the train rather than the car for long trips, and they roundly cheer the manufacturing of electric cars. Yet these same users of rail transport and "clean" cars are ready to protest against the production of electricity by gas-fired, coal-fired, oil-fired, or nuclear power plants, deemed (and justly so!) harmful to health and the environment.

As is often the case, the reality is more complex! In France, 70% of electricity is produced by nuclear power plants and 10% by hydraulic power stations. The remainder is delivered by coal-fired or gas-fired plants (10%) and by renewable energies, whether solar or wind (8%) and bioenergy (2%).

In France, if gasoline-fueled cars had to be replaced by electric cars, several (about fifteen?) nuclear power plants would probably have to be added to the existing network, which in turn would require heavy investments (more than a hundred billion euros). If nuclear energy is to be shunned, then many more gas-fired or coal-fired plants would be necessary. Now, their harmful effects on health and the environment are well known, especially with respect to miners and workers in processing plants.

To be sure, in manufacturing an electric car (as for a gasoline-fueled car) and in powering batteries, a lot of energy needs to be expended. Many minerals have to be extracted from the earth (iron, copper, manganese, nickel, gold, platinum, etc.) to create electronic parts and plastic components. Chemical substances have to be produced as well for batteries and paint. Finally, the transport, assembly, and recycling of all the parts, including the batteries, need to be added to the energy bill. In sum, a goodly amount of carbon monoxide will have been produced—which was touted as being saved at the start—in order to reduce greenhouse gases and global warming.[11] The concept of an "electric car" is without doubt nice on paper, but no solution is without drawback or flaw.

---

[11] See www.manicore.com. This excellent site by Jean-Marc Jancovici, recognized specialist on environmental matters, is a good starting point.

The Energy of Today and Tomorrow?

As we have seen, nothing is simple. All energy production and every mode of transportation, communication, construction, consumption habits, and so on generate some pollution, however slight, including that incurred through recycling. Endeavoring to eliminate, for example, the use of sulfur in motor fuels is a good thing, but the additional refining processes increase carbon dioxide emissions into the atmosphere. It is the final outcome that matters most, of course, so the eventual benefits should be calculated in the equation—both in terms of quantity (savings realized, etc.) and, if possible, quality (overall quality of the environment, with its positive impact on health, etc.). This reflection, complex in many ways, could be extended to other examples from everyday life. Is it better to use a dishwasher than to wash by hand? Variables such as the amount of water, electricity consumption, type of detergent, time saved, manufacturing, purchase, recycling, and replacement of the machine, etc., will all come into play, and the final "calculation" will not be so easy, especially in terms of savings (energy, financial, water, pollution, time, etc.).

The aim here is not to fundamentally question the sacrificial steps taken by communities, or the undeniable progress made by engineers in reducing energy usage. Developing "renewable" or "green" energies is certainly worthwhile, but it mustn't be forgotten that they are not always "clean" in the absolute sense or efficient, although significant progress has been made throughout the years.

Solar and wind energies, for instance, are intermittent and therefore tethered to more conventional energy sources such as gas, oil, or coal. The service life of wind turbines and solar panels is estimated to be about twenty to thirty years. These energies then raise new questions: What surface area and what investment should be allotted to them? What sort of "grey energy" is needed to produce them, to install them on site, to maintain them, and to ensure recycling takes place? It is for this reason that environmental activists speak today of "ecological transition." To drastically break away from nuclear energy, at least in France, does not seem realistic in the short term given the current standard of living (which is to be regretted), nor truly "environmental" to the extent that it would then be necessary to have recourse fossil fuels (such as lignite in Germany) and to accept an increase in the amount of CO_2 into the atmosphere.

Nuclear Energy

Should nuclear energy be trusted as "clean," since its production does not generate any carbon dioxide emission? And yet this remains to be demonstrated since energy, derived more often than not from fossil fuels, is required to build such plants. But this remains proportionally very low compared to the (atomic) energy produced by a nuclear power plant.

A good number of ecological movements and associations say, "No thanks!" to the proposition. The accident that occurred in 2011 at the Fukushima (Japan) nuclear plant, following a large-scale natural disaster (earthquake and tsunami), has called into question the use of this form of energy throughout the world. This has not, however, slowed down such projects underway in countries such as India, South Korea, and China (46 reactors in operation and 11 under construction in 2019, including two EPR-type reactors). Before the Japanese catastrophe, other countries such as Germany, Switzerland, or Belgium had already made a reasoned choice to reduce or to put an end altogether to nuclear power generation.

New technologies, however, are being studied. On the one hand, they aim to reduce uranium consumption (a hundred-year supply? This is also a limited fossil fuel!), notably by recycling plutonium derived from radioactive fuels already in use in customized plants (the fourth generation of sodium-cooled "fast neutrons" reactors) and by using depleted uranium (derived from natural uranium enrichment). But the backlogs in the construction and the implementation of these plants have somewhat dampened the promises that had been projected.

On the other hand, there is an attempt afoot to adapt nuclear *fusion* for civilian use. This is the goal of an international research project on the nuclear reactor Iter located in Cadarache, France.

Nuclear *fission* requires vast amounts of uranium ore (the first plants actually "burned" only about 5%) and produces just as much long-term radioactive waste.[12]

By contrast, thermonuclear *fusion*—made from two isotopes of hydrogen, deuterium (present, for example, in sea water at the rate of 33 mg per liter), and tritium (rare and radioactive, though it can be produced artificially)—would reduce waste by a considerable amount. And it would provide an even more powerful energy (four million times superior to chemical reactions such as coal, oil, or natural gas combustion), which is virtually inexhaustible, essentially harmless (*a priori* no risk of meltdown), and "clean" (no pollutant or greenhouse gases; the only by-product is helium, an inert and nontoxic gas). It is a matter of containing once again fire in its "solar" form (where the fusion is natural) and therefore nuclear. But this solution will take a long time to perfect (perhaps as long as a century, unless there is suddenly a major discovery) before producing a workable outcome on an industrial scale. Several research centers around the world are active in this field.

All these questions must be approached with foresight, a healthy critical distance, an expertise based on real facts (from the extraction of basic materials to the dismantlement and the recycling of materials after their use), and finally a genuine will to limit the different forms of pollution insofar as possible. This often boils down to choosing the "lesser evil" and often as well to choosing the "lowest cost," which is an undeniable restraint.

The Paradoxes of Wealth and Poverty

The great paradoxes of ecology, pollution, and the economy must be stated here. The wealthier the nation, the greater its ability

---

[12] This waste material is rated in France according to the activity level of the radioactive elements and their duration. They have a declining radioactivity over thousands or hundreds of thousands of years. High-activity (HA) wastes, the most hazardous, represent 0.2% of the total volume total of wastes but contain 98% of the radioactivity.

to abuse natural resources and to pollute the environment; while at the same time, its greater technical and financial means, supported in general by government regulations, can also combat and reduce the perverse effects of development on the environment. In the best-case scenario, what can be hoped for then is a course correction: the actual deterioration of environmental conditions will be gauged through the reaction time it takes between the development of a resource (extraction, processing, transport, etc.), the measurable pollution observed, and the implementation of adequate and efficient solutions in a reasonably short period of time on a human scale (a chemical or nuclear disaster, obviously, can pose long-term problems).

Conversely, the poorer the nation, the less likely it will be to develop its own resources, and the less likely it will have *a priori* an impact on nature. Nevertheless, sometimes the inhabitants of poor countries severely damage their environment through poorly managed farming practices (such as overgrazing and livestock left to wander and trample on plants, burn agriculture, or excessive logging). Their mineral resources are generally exploited by foreign businesses without their having any means of controlling the impact on their environment, and their most polluting industries (often outsourced) are not up to the standard of the anti-pollution norms in effect in wealthy nations. Finally, they struggle to overcome all of these difficulties for want of the financial, technical, and legislative means necessary for combatting the perverse effects of "underdevelopment" and for improving life circumstances. The effects of this "course deviation" on the environment are immediate. Work should then be done proactively to resolve or mitigate the causes of potential pollution and further damage.

The same is therefore true with respect to the exercise of human intelligence for resolving conflicts real and theoretical. Of course, Christians can contribute to this vast enterprise.

8

CHRISTIANS AND ECOLOGY

The Reformation inspired a number of Protestant intellectuals, poets, and scientists alike to treat nature as "the theater of God's glory," as Calvin coined the expression at the time. Over the course of the ensuing centuries, some of them joined initiatives led by other forerunners to heighten the awareness of their fellow citizens as to the importance of "preserving creation." This might explain in part why Northern European nations, influenced by Calvinism and Lutheranism, have been more sensitive to environmental issues than their Latin counterparts in the south, dominated as they were by Roman Catholicism. Yet, in the long run, the so-called Protestant work ethic led to a self-perpetuating prosperity that would often find itself at odds with environmental conservation efforts, although the very wealth created by these societies is ample proof that—were there a will to conserve—the means were never lacking.

Across the board, however, Christians have not reacted as urgently as might have been rightfully expected on their part, except for a few ecumenical conferences or theological roundtables where it was incumbent upon the participants to pay at least lip service to the issue. Otherwise, too many Christians have been slow to show interest and to propose the kind of solutions in keeping with their faith commitment.

Christians cannot brush aside this fact: An irresponsible attitude toward the environment can have negative repercussions on their witness to the world. How can nonbelievers—who live in society with them and observe them, up close or from afar—take them seriously when they show such little regard for sharing their blessings, when they take to the highways or the air in powerful machines that consume (and often waste) costly and highly polluting fuel? Many believers have allowed themselves to be carried away by the frenetic pace of consumerist society, without ever thinking of their struggling neighbors, including their brothers and sisters in the household of faith, who live in poverty at home and abroad; nor do they even consider their descendants on this earth, who just as much belong to the Lord. Nevertheless, as will be seen, this long indifference on the part of Christians has progressively been replaced by a real interest in environmental causes over the past thirty years.

The Major Conferences

The historic denominations followed the lead of secular international organizations by holding their first ecumenical conference in Vancouver in 1983 on the theme of "Justice, Peace, and Care for Creation," under the leadership of German physicist C. F. Von Weizsäcker. These conferences have then continued on a regular basis.

In 1989, the Conference of European Churches convened nearly six hundred delegates in Basel, Switzerland, on the same topic, reconvening in June 1997 in Graz, Austria. By the same token, the European Christian Environmental Network (ECEN) was established in 1998. This organization actually calls on Christian churches to celebrate a "Creation Season" with appropriate liturgies from the first Sunday in September to the second Sunday of October (see www.ecen.org).

First established in 1986 in Berne, the "Oeku—Church and Environment" movement brings together several parishes and Christian organizations with a view to "grounding more firmly with the life of the Church the message of its responsibility for creation care" (see https://www.oikoumene.org/en). Similar initiatives and organizations are sprouting up throughout Europe and the United States, in Protestant as well as in Catholic and Orthodox churches. In France, Catholics have been active establishing organizations, creating networks, and holding conferences to promote creation care. *Pax Christi* is one of the leading lights in this movement and since the 1980s has been proposing concrete steps for parishes to take in this endeavor (see www.paxchristi.cef.fr).

In June 2002 in Venice, Pope John-Paul II and the Orthodox patriarch, Bartholomew I, signed the *Common Declaration on Environmental Ethics*. Together, they recognized that "an awareness of the relationship between God and humankind brings a fuller sense of the importance of the relationship between human beings and the natural environment, which is God's creation and which God entrusted to us to guard with wisdom and love."

In 2015, Pope Francis published a significant encyclical titled *Laudato Si'* ("May you [the Lord] be praised!"), which drew on and synthesized documents produced by Episcopal conferences in numerous countries over the years to address the issue of creation care. Extending beyond the sphere of the Roman Catholic Church, this letter is addressed to men and women of good will the world over, inhabitants of our "shared home" that is in peril. But especially Christians are invited to live out an "ecological conversion" on the basis of their particular faith tradition.

More recently pursuant to this "conversion," an ecumenical initiative has popularized the "green church" branding. This is to say that local churches are invited to carry out their own "eco-diagnostic" in which they fill out a multiple-choice questionnaire based on five main themes: (1) liturgies and catechism (place accorded to creation care in prayer, sermons, catechism, etc.); (2) buildings (use and type of fuel, insulation, energy-saving measures, etc.); (3) grounds (showcasing of environmental values, farming, and biodiversity, etc.); (4) local and global engagement (information and teaching, events geared toward education concerning the environment and community action, etc.); and (5) lifestyle (means of transportation, recycling, saving and ethical investments, etc.).

Protestant and Evangelical Christians

Since 1961 in the United States, the Au Sable Environmental Institute—with its Protestant Evangelical Christian ethos, for many years under the leadership of Dr. Cal Dewitt—has offered scientific educational programs for students and adults of all ages (see www .ausable.org). Among the many new organizations on the scene is the Evangelical Environmental Network, which was behind the *Evangelical Declaration on Creation Care.* This declaration was later revised, adapted, and disseminated by the World Evangelical Alliance at its general assembly meeting in October 2008 (see www .creationcare.org).

The 1970 seminal work of Calvinist thinker Francis Schaeffer, *Pollution and the Death of Man,* offered without doubt one of the most vigorous defenses in favor of sound resource management and environmental protection to be found within Protestant and evangelical circles. Schaeffer built in particular on the work of Lynn White Jr., with whom he was much in agreement, though he better highlighted the fact that the Christian faith, when rightly understood and authentically lived out, leads to a concern for safeguarding the earth rather than allowing it to be abused.

In France, philosophers Jacques Ellul and Jean Brun worked to further increase awareness of environmental issues among church communities and even within the secular sphere. In particular, they critiqued the self-important scientism and technicism of modern societies, and they inveighed against the false sense of freedom and utopianism these are blindly expected to produce.

In 1987, evangelical Christians also met in Villars, Switzerland, to sign the *Declaration on Mutual Support and Development,* yet this text has often gone unnoticed. Several articles on the topic of environmentalism have been published since the 1970s, most notably by the theologian Henri Blocher.[1]

---

[1] See Henri Blocher, "Dieu est-il vert ?," *Fac-Réflexion,* no. 15 (January 1990); Philippe Gold-Aubert, "La pollution, ses dangers, ses limites," *Ichtus,* no. 40 (February 1974); Luc de Benoît and Jean Humbert, "La responsabilité écologique du chrétien," *Ichtus,* no. 50 (February-March 1975); *Écologie et Création* (articles by J. M. Daumas, H. Blocher, A.-G. Martin, C. H. Poizat, J. Brun, and P. Jones), *La Revue réformée,* no. 169 (June 1991), etc.

Evangelization and Creation Care

Beginning in 1974, the efforts of the Lausanne Movement have led evangelicals to become more cognizant of the close link between creation care in general and world evangelization in particular (see www.lausanne.org). In November 2012, this movement organized an international conference in Jamaica on the topic "Creation Care and the Gospel." Participants drafted a Call to Action with a preamble that invites Christians to reflect on how they might more actively participate in creation care. In 2016, they published the papers from this conference in *Creation Care and the Gospel: Reconsidering the Mission of the Church*.[2]

> Many of the world's poorest people, ecosystems, and species of flora and fauna are being devastated by violence against the environment in multiple ways, of which global climate change, deforestation, biodiversity loss, water stress, and pollution are but a part. We can no longer afford complacency and endless debate. Love for God, our neighbors, and the wider creation, as well as our passion for justice, compel us to "urgent and prophetic ecological responsibility."[3]

This text calls on Christians to adopt a simpler lifestyle, to revisit their theological teaching on creation care, to encourage the entire church to fight against climate change, to promote the principles of sustainable food production, as well an economic development in harmony with God's creation, and finally to introduce means of environmental protection favoring biodiversity on a local level:

---

[2] Colin Bell and Robert S. White, eds., *Creation Care and the Gospel: Reconsidering the Mission of the Church* (Peabody, MA: Hendrickson, 2016).

[3] See https://www.lausanne.org/fr/mediatheque/compte-rendu-de-consultation/evangile-et-protection-de-lenvironnement-appel-a-laction (translation F. Baudin).

We welcome all projects and actions in the Church at large
with environmental protection in view, though they might be
qualified as "small beginnings" or "symbolic gestures." They
nevertheless serve as poignant a witness to our common faith
in Jesus Christ, the Lord of creation. . . . Finally, we wish to
express our convictions with humility and respect.

Christian Action on the Ground

In 1983 in Great Britain, an organization called *A Rocha* ("The
Rock" in Portuguese) was created by Pastor Peter Harris and his
wife Miranda, along with two close friends, Les and Wendy Batty.
From the beginning, they were supported by John Stott, a well-
known Anglican priest with evangelical leanings and a passionate
ornithologist (he also happened to be one of the main movers and
shakers behind the Lausanne Movement).

Peter Harris moved his family to Algarve in southern Portugal
to establish an environmental protection project undergirded by a
specifically Christian perspective. He inaugurated the first welcome
and study center dedicated to preserving the Alvor Estuary, which
was threatened at that time by real estate development proposals for
touristic purposes. This estuary contained many protected flora and
fauna, and the inhabitants of the region used it to harvest a portion
of their food supply. The work of *A Rocha* proved instrumental in
preserving this exceptional site.[4]

Near the end of the 1990s, *A Rocha* took on an international
dimension. The organization can now boast of over twenty chapters located on several continents: Great Britain, Kenya, Lebanon,
France, Czech Republic, Canada, India, Peru, United States, Ghana,
and so on (see www.arocha.org). The primary "mission" of each
local chapter is to raise awareness among Christians and non-
Christians alike about the need to protect the environment and to

---

[4] See Peter Harris, *Foi d'Ecolo* (Marne-la-Vallée: Farel, 2005).

establish, wherever possible, scientific ventures designed to restore ecosystems under threat.

In France, *A Rocha* was established in 2000 and set up in 2003 a welcome and environmental study center in the Baux-de-Provence valley near Arles (south of France, between Marseille and Montpellier). Their team of scientists, professionals, and volunteers set to work first in residual wetlands, which are remnants of once abundant marshlands, some of which are now protected by the "Natura 2000" network. As one of the last remaining marshlands of the valley, it has been classified as a nature reserve. This is thanks in large part to the work of *A Rocha*, which manages this space in collaboration with the regional Nature Park of the Alpilles on behalf of the French Coastal Protection Agency. The organization had to give up this first center, but the research and conservation project continues in this valley with its exceptional ecological heritage. However, *A Rocha France* has accepted responsibility for managing another remarkable ecological site, the *Domaine des Courmettes*, whose buildings are currently being renovated, located on the heights overlooking the French Riviera. A professional team, under the direction of Jean-François Mouhot, ensures the scientific monitoring of this estate of several hundred hectares. It welcomes groups and individuals to raise their awareness of ecological issues through seminars, conferences, field visits, and so on. Emphasis is placed on the need for each person to change his or her lifestyle in order to reduce environmental damage. For Christians, prayer accompanies this effort to safeguard creation, in close connection with the training aimed at reconciling faith and ecology, given on the spot and in the churches and various biblical and theological institutions.

More recently, based on the "Eco-Church" model proposed by *A Rocha* in 2016 in association with several churches and NGOs in Great Britain, the "Green Church" label was launched on an ecumenical initiative to accompany "ecological conversion" (the term seems to us a little strong, even out of place; it rather designates the logical consequence of conversion to God). Local churches are invited to make an "eco-diagnosis" by filling in a multiple-choice questionnaire covering five themes: celebrations and catechesis (place of the care for creation in prayer, preaching, and catechesis, etc.), buildings (energy, insulation, and saving measures, etc.), land (ecological enhancement, biodiversity, etc.), local and global commitment (information and teaching, environmental awareness events, community actions, etc.), and lifestyles (modes of travel, waste recycling, ethical savings and investments, etc.). This label is useful to invite Christians to reflect and act at the "parish" or "community" level (see www.ecochurch.arocha.org.uk).

A Humanitarian and Environmental "Mission"

Some organizations, such as the *Service d'Entraide et de Liaison* (SEL, Service of Mutual Support and Partnership), established by the French Evangelical Alliance (AEF) in 1980, have been able to draw the attention of evangelical Christians and Protestants in France to the importance of promoting sustainable development in the Global South. SEL financed and supported many sustainable development projects, albeit on a modest (but very effective!) scale, though principally in Francophone Africa. This organization relies on a network of Protestant and evangelical churches to plan and execute these projects, and it makes a point of refraining from any favoritism in terms of which specific ethnic groups receive aid.

Through its partner association, Artisan-SEL, Christians were also able to participate (until 2018) in an ambitious "sustainable business" project, which may seem somewhat utopian: to engage in commence and to consume goods in such a way as to "reduce inequalities and restore Man to his rightful place in international trade." The sustainable trade project draws on Article 23 of the Universal Declaration of Human Rights, adopted by the United Nations General Assembly in 1948: "Everyone who works has the right to just and favourable remuneration ensuring for himself and his family an existence worthy of human dignity."

This new model of commerce therefore aims to stabilize business transactions so as to satisfy both the supplier and the consumer. A more equitable compensation for the work of producers and artisans—often some of the most disadvantaged members of the classic economic system—allows these to meet their basic needs in the realms of health, education, housing, and social welfare. The fundamental rights of individuals must be respected by the proponents of sustainable trade, notably when it comes to prohibiting child labor and any other forms of slavery and religious or ethnic discrimination. Again, this initiative has to do with prioritizing better working conditions and business relationships over the long term. But organic farming and environmental conservation also feature prominently among the key elements of this approach (see www.selfrance.org).

On the world stage, SEL has chosen to support the "Micah Challenge" (now Micah Global), in reference to the prophet Micah in the Bible, who encourages God's people to practice righteousness and to take pleasure in manifesting, with humility, the goodness inspired by God on a daily basis, especially toward the weakest (Mic. 6:8). This worldwide movement, which brings together nearly 800 member organizations in 90 countries, offers Christians the opportunity to mobilize against poverty among other things through advocacy actions aimed at challenging political authorities. Micah Global supports one of the objectives set by the United Nations in 2000: "To reduce poverty by half by 2015, based on key poverty indicators." For all Christians, this laudable goal is above all in conformity with the teachings of Moses and the prophets, as well as with those of Jesus and the apostles. The sharing of resources need not be a hollow slogan, for Christians of every stripe are called to be "the salt of the earth"—to provide a bit of flavor and true "rest" or peace for this world. If they wish to speak against injustice, their behavior should also conform as much as possible to the ideal evangelical model, as defined by Jesus in the Sermon on the Mount (Matt. 5–7). The Micah Challenge and SEL call on Western Christians to adopt a simpler lifestyle. There can be little doubt that this can lead to a *healthier* (in the broadest and most practical sense of the term) relationship with the environment (see https://www.micahnetwork.org).

Environment and Development

Development in the Southern Hemisphere has become the subject of deep rethinking among both Christians and non-Christians, based on the experience of the past thirty years. Most, if not all, of the private and public humanitarian organizations are now convinced that it is simply naive to throw money at problems. It is likewise useless to flood the markets of developing nations with food products originating from developed countries unless, of course, it is designated for disaster relief (drought, earthquakes, tsunamis, etc.) or in the case of local or international political conflict (which actually occurs more frequently). The risk is that developing countries become dependent on developed countries and become "addicted" to counting on aid, which then becomes a fixed feature of their economic system, rather than relying on their own resources for finding local and sustainable solutions.

The drawbacks of traditional aid have now been identified. First of all, massive financial aid (or long-term "loans") often engenders a debt that is impossible to reimburse. Second, food aid can change the habits of local populations and increase their dependence on these goods, such as bread made with wheat flour, which may not always be produced on site. Third, food aid can also upset local markets, notably by devaluing the products of local farmers. Finally, any kind of aid can even serve as a political tool in the event of local conflicts, when one faction appropriates it to the detriment of other ethnicities or clans in a country or region.

The various humanitarian international organizations today believe that the relationship between the local, human, and natural environment is critical. They realize that sustainable development hinges on support measures (economic and agricultural advice, for example), as well as incentive measures (microloans and various forms of financing), so that the target populations might be able to implement *their own means of development*. The solution to certain problems, such as controlling demographic growth, has to include education (literacy, hygiene awareness, introduction to family management, etc.), in particular for young women. Emphasis is also laid on aiding child sponsorship so as to give the young the possibility of receiving an education, at least at the elementary level, under conditions acceptable both for themselves and their families.

Tailored programs can be integrated into mission projects, and these often have tangible results. On that score and on the basis of sound biblical teaching, Christians in developing nations have been encouraged to plant market gardens and to start farms, but with a real know-how in their management that also respects the environment. Moreover, an effort has been made to improve living standards and working conditions, while at the same time promote ethical debate and the implementation of appropriate legislation in order to protect the most at-risk workers, in particular in the field of mineral extraction.

In African nations, where the agricultural sector is especially predominant (often from 70% to 80% of the population), development programs have incorporated active measures of environmental protection, notably for promoting soil restoration and sustainable agriculture.

Hope for the Earth

Two other initiatives led by Protestants have played a pioneering role, as extraordinary as they are exemplary, in Tunisia under the guidance of Abel and Jane Granier (from 1953 to 1969) and in Burkina Faso (West Africa) with Henri and Marthe Girard (since 1987). Although their lay work is inspired by Christian faith and values, it benefits a large segment of the population of diverse ethnic and religious backgrounds. It is also based on a sound understanding of natural and human settings, gained through practical experience on the ground and in direct contact with local communities.

The main merit of these innovators is to improve local farming techniques, some of which are age-old, while delving even deeper into tradition thanks to knowledge developed by consulting the earliest records—such as Abel Granier, who consulted the writings of Punic and Roman authors! They likewise draw on personal experience. For instance, Henri Girard, who is the son of a farmer from the Avesnois "bocage" (fields surrounded by hedges) in the north of France, recreated this very specific wooded space in the Sahel region,[5] taking the advice or accepting the help of experts or foreign and local volunteer interns, which included agronomists, botanists, technicians, and so on.

Their line of work (in which they are certainly not alone) is convincing and encouraging proof that it is indeed possible to restore soils in areas previously deemed irredeemable. This means that it is possible to mitigate the effects of desertification and climate change and to practice a productive, organic, and sustainable form of agriculture, which adequately provides food for entire households (see www.eauterreverdure.org and www.abelgranier.net).

In Burkina Faso, in villages that participate in the work of the pilot farm Guié (which is now managed by the inhabitants themselves), the yield of cereals such as millet or sorghum has tripled or quadrupled by adopting some relatively simple measures based on the "bocage" model. These include using "improved zaï" techniques,[6] composting, small dikes for storm-water retention, crop rotation to replenish the soils in natural nitrogen, fallowing, and managed grazing, and so forth. Other measures require more collective cooperation, such as creating reservoirs for the control of surface runoff, irrigation, and the replenishment of water tables; planting hedgerows (key system components) to strengthen dikes and enclosures (which are regularly pruned to provide firewood for cooking) and to protect fields from damage caused by roaming

---

[5] The Sahel is that semiarid transitional zone in Africa between the Sahara Desert to the north and the humid savannas to the south.—Trans.

[6] Zaï consists of digging holes about 30 cm in diameter and 15 to 20 cm deep during the dry season. The farmers deposit a little ripe compost in these holes, then they cover it with a small amount of soil. At the edge of these covered holes, they are able to sow grain as soon as the first rains come, which would otherwise be judged insufficient if this technique was not used. The water collects in the fertilized hole, which is enough to provide good conditions for the seed to germinate before more abundant rains occur and nourish the developing plant.

domestic animals or wild beasts; laying out communication routes, delimited by the planting of roadside trees, to ensure access to fields and to facilitate traffic between villages, and so on.

These measures, which are undertaken each time on a village-wide scale (a dozen communities of about 1,000 inhabitants are concerned in the region of Guiè), can be extended to the technical and farming sectors (nurseries for the reproduction of seed, tree, and shrub planting, maintenance workshops for machines, etc.) and especially to the social sphere (welcome and aid to women about to give birth, child care and orphan services, clinics for basic health needs, training of farmers, "woodlands school," etc.). Several pilot farms have now been established in the country.[7] Another project, which looks very promising and has already borne fruit, was launched in Mali. Other farms inspired by the method and the techniques used in Guiè have been set up in neighboring countries. One of the most positive effects of this work has also been to stem the rural exodus toward large overpopulated cities where unemployment, poverty, and violence are the day-to-day reality of many migrants, and that against the backdrop of the dire health risks found in extremely rundown and polluted urban settings. It cannot be excluded that this may also have positive effects on migration.

Lastly, these many endeavors—which have proliferated these past several years in Christian "missions" and other religious or lay organizations, whether private (NGOs) or public (see, for example, www.iedafrique.org)—demonstrate that local communities can indeed care for themselves and also participate actively in their own development. If external assistance, especially financial in nature, remains indispensable for initiating and expanding these projects, then the self-motivation of communities remains critical for ensuring a sustainable development that is at the same time environmentally friendly. This is true as much in developing nations as in developed ones. On this score, Christians certainly have every reason to find a resource in their faith tradition and spiritual heritage.

---

[7] See Frederic Baudin, *Greening the Sahel, Land Restoration in West Africa: Conversations with Henri Girard* (Aix-en-Provence, France: CEM, 2017), English Kindle version (www.amazon.com).

An Innovative Motivation

Two crucial questions remain: What will motivate us to desire to live more temperately and to behave more justly, out of respect for God and love for our neighbors, in particular for the poorest among them? How can we find the will to protect and transmit a natural heritage that can enable future generations to live in the best possible conditions?

Some seem to think that we can derive motivation through fear of a worldwide political conflict, a nuclear meltdown, a major industrial accident causing the irreversible destruction of nature on a massive scale, or a large-scale natural disaster due to climate change (now unequivocally verified in its effects), pandemics, and so on.[8] Obviously, all of these eventualities are eminently possible, even probable, for they are already a lived reality in some quarters. When the worst does happen, believers know that God is sovereign and that he sustains the world. It must simply be observed that human beings make questionable life choices, which are not without consequences for their neighbors and on their environment.

Fearmongering is all the rage these days, yet it is highly doubtful that this is the most efficacious way to stimulate people to change their lifestyles. It is true that people make some wise decisions out of fear; for example, when they stop themselves from stepping off a cliff and plunging to their death. While fear can obvious pedagogical value, it is also said that fear is "a poor counselor"—nor is fear the best of motivators when wielded by political authorities, no more than the oppressive force of a tyrannical state in indoctrinating citizens or compelling them to obey. This is also the case for any moralizing and guilt-ridden speech to that end. Ecological catastrophe, which today has its most zealous or radical "prophets,"

---

[8] This precision is added by the author at a time when the Covid-19 epidemic is spreading across all continents (April 2020) and will have definite effects on the people, the environment, and the economy around the world.

sometimes very young, is not always based on rational arguments. It rarely leads to a constructive attitude. If one really wanted to frighten people and probably obtain immediate effects, one could imagine coloring carbon dioxide, ozone, or methane in fluorescent red; the reaction would be spectacular! But this is hardly conceivable, nor even probably desirable.

It is more advantageous to resort to positive values and realistic ways that are universal in appeal, such as the enjoyment of living in a less-polluted environment and the freedom from the enslavement of the extravagant standards of modern society. These values also invite people to accept basic responsibility and not to systematically rely on external aid, whether public or private, except when necessary for the most vulnerable. Every system of social welfare (health, unemployment, retirement, etc.) can function as long as each person feels free and accountable to establish, maintain, and make proper use of it. When there is abuse, it is possible to speak of "overuse" and "social pollution," with the concomitant negative effects for the human and natural environment.

Faith, however, offers an additional resource—which is without doubt foundational—for better living in this world. In his 2007 work, *La ferme des voyants* (*The Farm of the Seers*), Abel Granier, who was a Reformed pastor (he also had a doctorate in law and in theology and was a specialist of Semitic languages), emphasized many times over that his Christian faith, grounded in a close reading of the Bible with a high view of its divine inspiration, has been critical for carrying out his work, at times in the worst human or agricultural conditions and in the most troubled political circumstances. It was through his faith that he found both the freedom and the nerve to restore soils thought unrecoverable for local agriculture; and it was through his faith that he found the courage to go against the grain of prevailing ideologies.[9] Similarly, when he talks about the difficulties he encountered in setting up a bocage in Burkina Faso, Henri Girard says,

---

[9] Abel Granier, *La ferme des voyants* (Paris: Société des Écrivains, 2007), see esp. ch. 5 and pp. 79, 81, 141–42, 204ff.

My faith has helped me, from a personal point of view, to accomplish this project. My motivation has deepened. I have drawn new strength and inspiration from it and that has given more meaning to my initial commitment, particularly my desire to see human beings live more harmoniously with the natural environment they are called to cultivate and conserve.[10]

Apart from any responsibility that may indeed be attributed to individual Christians for the ecological crisis, apart from any admission of failure even partial on their part in this domain, faith can inspire Christians and orient them in a positive manner, as long as they learn how to live out their faith on a daily basis and in a practical way.

Trust and Providence

This authentic motivation first takes the form of an increased *trust* placed in a providential God who "will meet all your needs according to the riches of his glory in Christ Jesus" (Phil. 4:19). Trusting in God by counting on him for the present age and the age to come becomes clearer as time goes by. It is necessary to *learn* how to better "know" the "Father, the Almighty, creator of heaven and earth," and to better understand his word, the Bible, which enables us to grasp his will on this earth that he wants to protect and keep. There is a fine line to respect: when individuals desire to cultivate the land without protecting it, they run the risk of destroying it; and if they neglect to cultivate it, out of excessive concern for protecting it, they risk starvation.

It takes time to learn how to live in a more intimate communion with the Father, thanks to the ever-present mediation of his Son Jesus, the Messiah crucified and resurrected who enables all to turn away from evil and sin and to choose good and life. It also takes time for the Holy Spirit to bring about the maturation pro-

---

[10] See Baudin, *Greening the Sahel*.

cess in the life of all those who place their trust in the Godhead, constituted by the *fruits* of his presence: love, joy, peace, patience, goodness, and so on (Gal. 5:22; 1 Cor. 13:4). Now if these fruits are abundant in the life of believers, then they will not remain inactive in the present world—namely, to care for other human beings as well as for creation as a whole. In principle, the more believers cultivate and keep communion with God, the better they tend to cultivate and keep his "garden."

The providence of God enables those who can discern it in this world to face the future with greater confidence. God already restores the life of those who entrust themselves to him; he leads them in the ways of truth, righteousness, and love. He allows them to discover the pathways of an authentic freedom, albeit still relative in this world, as it is lived out "under grace" (Rom. 6). The protection of the environment must not become a new fundamentalist religion, inflexible in its blind dogmatism, with its priests and priestesses devoted to the cult of *Gaia* (the Earth) and imposing their ecological dictate on this earth and its inhabitants; this tyrannical "ecologism," rooted in the "green utopia" aimed at "saving the planet" (as we already see and hear it everywhere in this world) could quickly become similar to deadly ideologies, the effects of which are well known. Just as it is important to become wise and prudent producers and consumers, it also remains possible, by leaning on God, to live carefree and guilt-free.

This trust in God is the first step toward a "corrective action" in this world. It is enriched by the experience of the faithfulness of God as much during periods of prosperity as during times of crisis. Faith is finally the precondition for being able to act with a certain lightheartedness, which in turn leads to a logical plan of action: having first God in view, then other human beings, and finally nature itself that "surrounds"[11] us.

It is therefore possible, through faith, to put into action at least three steps for better "exercising dominion and subduing"

---

[11] The French verb here is *environner* and is meant by the author to invoke the environment.—Trans.

creation as good stewards who are responsible and joyful, serious and informed.

Resisting Temptation

The first step is simply to resist the temptations of modern civilization. This is, of course, in line with traditional Christian teaching and serves also as the most basic and practical approach to environmental issues.

Resistance consists in refraining from exercising an abusive dominance over nature by means of a more and more efficient, powerful technology and through exorbitant financial expenditures. Today, it is possible to do almost anything when promoting human health, improving nutrition, enhancing living standards, developing modes of transport, shortening travel times, controlling human existence from the moment of conception, designing extraordinary software tools and using "artificial intelligence," probing the universe, and so on.

"Everything is permissible!" In the first century, the Christians in Corinth took up this catchphrase, which today finds its echo in the slogan "No Limits!" to justify egocentric behavior. The catchphrase, however, is immediately qualified by the apostle Paul, who adds, "but not everything is beneficial." More to the point, Paul explains that he will not let himself "be mastered by anything" (1 Cor. 6:12 CSB). When the full text is considered, these are sound words to live by, from which Christians of every age can draw inspiration. Paul provides the model, to which he himself bears witness:

> I have learned to be content whatever the circumstances. I know what it is to be in need, and I know what it is to have plenty. I have learned the secret of being content in any and every situation, whether well fed or hungry, whether living in plenty or in want. I can do all this through him who gives me strength. (Phil. 4:11–13)

As a follow-up to this resistance to temptation, a willingness to refrain from any unwarranted transgression vis-à-vis human limits must be added. Restraint can be defined as accepting with resignation these limits, and thus suppressing the will to power that manifests itself in (among other things,) uncontrolled consumption. Although the latter is constantly stoked by the pervasiveness of advertising, behavior modification can overcome this. Faced with the onslaught of invasive and self-serving marketing strategies, a critical perspective is thus very much *de rigueur*. It is not always easy to contend, however, with the disinformation disseminated in the modern world, where all sorts of data gushes forth—some true, some false, most unverifiable—to justify at times conflicting propositions whose implications for society are far from certain. And what about the "psychological pollution" that is spreading through increasingly sophisticated surveillance networks (cameras, radars, satellites, Internet "cookies," facial recognition systems, etc.), tracking individuals in their life choices, movements, consumption patterns, and even in their intimacy, under the pretext of better apprehending offenders, who nevertheless represent only a small minority of the population? Our technological environment must not become an area of enslavement, thanks to the most efficient tools (which are moreover dangerous in the event of a political slide toward a totalitarian system) imagined and created by human beings. It is a fact that the multiplication of computer systems, networks, and screens, which are voracious in energy and raw materials, is detrimental to the quality of our physical environment. Is it really indispensable, and ultimately so reassuring, to be observed in this way at all hours of the day and night in our cities in order to prevent the risk of delinquency? Or to help us control people and their health in the event of an epidemic? Is it necessary to constantly increase the speed of data transmission to make these "connected" networks (including for private purposes) more efficient? These questions remain unanswered. Accepting a share of risk in our hyper-connected and secure societies remains undoubtedly necessary for life to express itself more freely, without excluding the responsibility of each person, which leads to respect for all. A fine ideal, so often contradicted by reality, if we are aware of it! In any case, it seems wise to be wary of the "systems" that hinder this freedom, and of the deep springs within the human being that call it into question. All this is also part of our "environment."

An Iconoclastic Attitude

Nothing is more biblical, then, than to resolve to cast down the tyrannical idol of wealth and to learn how to be "content" (Paul's word) with what is necessary rather than superfluous for living. It must be recognized, though, that this distinction is not always easy to make and put into practice. Is it healthy to work to the point of not knowing how to relax? Is it really necessary to choose a beach half a world away to sunbathe and swim, when our own coastlines and shorelines offer so many landscapes that tourists the world over envy and wish to visit? On the other hand, it is true that a sojourn in far removed countries, when "smart" and environmentally friendly, can afford local communities the opportunity for a better standard of living.

Without doubt, Christians would do well to pray for themselves the prayer of Augur: "Keep falsehood and lies far from me; give me neither poverty nor riches, but give me only my daily bread" (Prov. 30:8). As for rest, it also would be well for them to remind themselves of the Solomonic psalm: "In vain you rise early and stay up late, toiling for food to eat—for he [God] grants sleep to those he loves" (Ps. 127:2).

Anchored in the knowledge that Christ strengthens their faith, Christians can return to a more sober and more just lifestyle, true to the teachings of the prophets and the apostles in the Bible (Ps. 73; Jer. 9:22–24; Ezek. 27–28; 1 Thess. 5:6; James 5:1–6). Motivated by faith, and not by fear, they can learn how to live in the present age, though with an eye cast on the future, both near and far. They can work to save the natural resources of the earth by reducing their consumption of energy (gasoline, gas, electricity), drinking water and food, pesticides (including those for home gardens), and leisure activities (choice of holiday destinations, ecotourism, etc.). They can assume their share of responsibility, which is more necessary today than ever in developed countries, to reduce meat consumption whose production poses a particular environmental threat linked to animal feed (water and fodder crops). It is not imperative, however, to become a vegetarian on that account. After all, after Noah survived the flood, God gave him permission to consume plants and animals. Paul also confirms this stance on eating meat in his letters.

Lastly, Christians know that there is (and that there will be) no perfect ecology. They do not believe that human beings—as a result of their remarkable intelligence, amazing technical know-how, or even their best measures for protecting the environment and ensuring sustainable development—will be able to establish the kingdom of God on earth. For them, it is not a question of "saving the planet" and its inhabitants from a strictly materialistic or idealistic perspective, although they lucidly assess the current situation and the urgency of certain measures to be taken. Rather, it is important to them that human beings, in their spiritual component, be saved by their faith in God the Savior, so that they may then safeguard, as far as possible and without panic, this earth they share with their fellow human beings. Their iconoclastic attitude leads them to view the world with a critical eye, while remaining positive and optimistic.

Discernment and Creativity

The second step is for Christians to engage more in critical thinking, exercising both their human and their spiritual discernment skills, so that as a result they might dare to question the prevailing paradigms. Christians are often called to swim against the tide. Such was the case of Daniel and his deported companions in sixth-century BC Babylon. This truth is also in keeping with the exhortation of Paul gave to Christians under the Roman Empire: "Do not be conformed to this world, but be transformed by the renewal of your mind, that by testing you may discern what is the will of God, what is good and acceptable and perfect" (Rom. 12:2 ESV).

Paul's entreaty follows on the heels of his call to be a "living sacrifice" (Rom 12:2 ESV). This also implies a certain nonconformity (though remaining respectful of civic authority and public institutions as he states in Rom. 13) at the same time as a "transformation." For believers live in the present world while simultaneously enjoying citizenship in the new order inaugurated by Christ. The verbs used here by Paul are in the passive voice in Greek, demonstrating that transformation is the work of God himself, though that it cannot be completed without the assent of the individual believer. This veritable metamorphosis should lead Christians to see the world and their neighbors in a new light, not to mention to conduct themselves in a manner that conforms to the mind of God in all that is "good and acceptable, and perfect."

It is to be noted that this change first takes place in the understanding, followed by the heart that is moved and transformed by the Spirit of God. The mind and the will are henceforth reoriented so that the physical and spiritual relationship of believers with the world is entirely renewed. It is certainly here that a new connection between the human and natural environment can be formed, with all the positive effects (yet not without tension) that might be expected.

Lastly, it is not a stretch to read between the lines a real encouragement in this passage, addressed as much to the individual believer as to the entire Christian community: the discernment necessary for knowing the will of God can be learned, thanks to the common exercise of gifts when believers are brought together, truly forming the "body" of Christ, as indicated by the apostle Paul.

One of the outcomes of this new relationship with the world should be the development of a type of creativity. Christians, without being the only ones of course, should have the freedom and boldness to actively participate in research for new solutions in all areas of life in society, while at the same time respecting the fundamental limits of biblical ethics. Here again, nothing is ever simple when it comes to understanding the issues at hand and developing the resourcefulness necessary for discovering sustainable solutions. There is thus a place for Christian leaders to devote their energies to encourage young people in their congregations to strike out with confidence (and competence) in the research field and scientific endeavors—always buttressed, of course, by their trust in an almighty and providential God.

There are certainly other beneficial by-products being overlooked here of the spiritual education of mobilizing believers to better exercise *dominion* over the earth while *protecting* it as a real *service*. In any event, this should lead them to propose alternative models that do not operate according to the same ethical rules in effect in secular society. Their initiatives could provide crucial momentum for a reasonable and shared development that respects both humankind and the environment.

Practically speaking, a good starting place would be to abide by the oft-cited rule of the four "Rs": Reduce, Reuse, Recycle, Rethink. Each term deserves further development, though it will suffice here to imagine, were they to be truly followed, how they might impact daily life, not to mention other domains such as the habitat, transportation, the food supply, and so on. It's good to start by asking relevant questions before acquiring this or that thing or starting a new activity: such as whether it's necessary, urgent, and useful; whether we don't already have it in a similar form, and so on. This ethical questioning, which is akin to the search for a certain compromise or the "lesser evil," must not however become an unbearable puzzle, a permanent obsession.

Education and Raising Awareness

The third step consists in focusing on education in churches so as to raise environmental awareness, especially among the youth. This can begin within the framework of a Sunday school program or catechism, where young people are reminded of the biblical foundations for creation care and where respect for the environment is inculcated. The same approach can obviously apply to adult Christian education programs. Special-interest Christian organizations (such as the Micah Project or *A Rocha*) could be prevailed upon to give lectures or lead nature walks. It is always more impactful in understanding the true sense of the term "biodiversity" when on the ground; and it is often while studying plant and animal species (identifying them either by their scientific nomenclature or familiar names) that people can develop an interest in better protecting them.

It is always possible to broach the topic of environmentalism within the Christian community at an open forum, when practical solutions can be sought for saving energy during a church renovation or construction project. It is always helpful to compare diverse points of view and consider different life experiences, so that church members can make prudent choices about regular activities such as communal meals, travel distance to meetings, or the possibility of sharing resources among multiple communities (buildings, personnel, etc.). This is what it means to be a "Green Church." In considering resource use, a "Green Church" is also mindful of fellow believers in the Global South—namely, those on the frontlines who are more closely threatened by climate change.

Raising awareness is certainly not a matter of engaging in a narrow and unyielding moralism, but rather of promoting an "enthusiastic ecology" or "passionate environmentalism." That would be the fruit of a living relationship with God, an attitude that is respectful of the environment, free and responsible, by grace. One could consider it as a way of life founded on a "cheerful restraint" and an "informed and confident consumerism" by faith in the one God—Father, Son, and Holy Spirit—from whom all things come and for whom all things are (1 Cor. 8:6; Col. 1:12–20). In the final analysis, it is up to each individual believer, living alone or in community, solidly planted in the present world but with eyes fixed on the world to come, to put into practice the greatest of commandments to love God and to love neighbor.